Finding God in the World

An Introduction to
Josef Pieper's Sacramental Worldview

Fr. Christopher Seith

En Route Books and Media, LLC
Saint Louis, MO

⊕ENROUTE
Make the time

En Route Books and Media, LLC
5705 Rhodes Avenue
St. Louis, MO 63109

Cover credit: Joni Seith, using an Icon painted by Saint Gregory of Sinai Monastery, Kelseyville, CA

Copyright © 2025 Christopher Seith

ISBN-13: 979-8-88870-459-2
Library of Congress Control Number:
Available online at https://catalog.loc.gov

Scripture texts in this work are taken from the *New American Bible, revised edition* © 2010, 1991, 1986, 1970 Confraternity of Christian Doctrine, Washington, D.C. No permission necessary for use of fewer than 5,000 words of the NAB in which such use comprises less than 40% of a single book of the Bible and less than 40% of the proposed work.

All Rights Reserved. No part of this book may be reproduced, stored in a retrieval system, or transmitted in any form, or by any means, electronic, mechanical, photocopying, or otherwise, without the prior written permission of the author or publisher.

Dedication

To the Theotokos,
whose presence in my life
has made the ideas expressed in this book
a living reality for me.

Front Cover Explanation

The icon depicted on the front cover is known as "Platytera ton Ouranon," which in Greek means, "More Spacious than the Heavens." Mary is seen bearing the Infinite God in her womb as her hands are raised in prayer for the world. Christ, the Incarnate Word of God, teaches and blesses the world (as is seen from the scroll he holds) by hiding himself within His creature. In some ways, the whole of this book is contained in this icon. In Pieper's words: "thought and word must retain in its purity the link with the image...; without the image, thought and word have no historical effectiveness. It is not the 'idea' of bravery, but the image, the symbol (lion, eagle, banner) that has a direct effect; not the conceptually formulated idea of love, but the image of the pelican nourishing its young with its own blood. The Word, the Logos of God, becomes effective in history by being born 'of Mary,' becoming a visible person; and Mary, although less powerful than her offspring, remains the mediatrix."[1]

---

[1] Josef Pieper, *Exercises in the Elements: Essays — Speeches — Notes*, trans. Daniel Farrelly (South Bend: St. Augustine's Press, 2019), 75.

Acknowledgments

I was first introduced to Pieper's work during my time in seminary in a class on the virtues, taught by Sr. Catherine Joseph Droste, OP, at the Angelicum in Rome. That class, together with the overall atmosphere of the seminary and the relationships fostered during my time in Rome, awakened in me an insatiable thirst for the wisdom I found in Pieper's writings. I am deeply indebted to the teachers, formators, and brother seminarians whom I encountered during that time. Particular mention must be made of my classmates, Fr. Jim Hinkle, Fr. Patrick Broussard, Fr. Jeremy Theis, and Fr. Garrett Nelson, whose classroom antics played an indispensable role in my intellectual formation.

I am also deeply grateful for my brother priests who have encouraged me in the never-ending pursuit of wisdom. In particular, I am grateful for Fr. Patrick Lewis, Fr. Jamie Morrison, Fr. Brendan Glasgow, Fr. Carter Griffin, and Fr. Ben Petty. Their fraternity and priestly witness is a continual source of encouragement.

There are many religious sisters who, in so many ways, embody Mary's presence for me. Without their presence in my life, the sacramentality of the Church would have remained an abstract idea. I will never be able to adequately express my gratitude for their vocation, which is such a support for my own. I am especially grateful to the nuns of Christ the Bridegroom Monastery and St. Dominic's Monastery, and the religious sisters of the Religious Sisters of Mercy and the Servants of the Lord.

This book began as a book for seminarians at the request of the Institute for Priestly Formation (whose presence in my life continues to bless me in so many ways). Despite its shift in focus, this book has been shaped by the seminarians of St. John Paul II Seminary in more ways than they can know. Wisdom is found in dialogue alone. By the questions they have asked and the homilies and conferences they have received with such excitement, my own understanding of Pieper's wisdom has been refined. Above all, they have formed my heart into that of a father and so have taught me how God communicates his Wisdom to his children.

Finally, I am grateful to my parents, my sister, Fr. Scott Valentyn, Mother Gabriella, Mother Natalia, and Colette, all of whom read various versions of the book throughout the writing process. Without their encouragement (and pestering!), I would not have persevered in writing this book. It is only their excitement for Pieper's insights and their desire for me to write this book that made it possible for me to do so. Even more, it is their love and care that have made this work not only a "work," but truly a labor of love.

Table of Contents

Acknowledgments i

Introduction 1

Chapter 1: Beholding Christ 9

    Contemplation and Wonder 16

    Contemplation of God in Human Misery 20

    Contemplation and Transcendence of Self 24

    The Contemplative Christian 31

Chapter 2: Becoming Christ 35

    The Christian Idea of Man 42

    Prudence 48

    Justice 54

    Fortitude 60

    Temperance 66

Chapter 3: Embodying Christ 75

    Flourishing through Love 81

    The Visibility of Divine Love 84

    Acedia and the Flight from Divine Beauty 91

    The Sacredness of Creation 97

    Silence: The Final Revelation 100

    Conclusion 104

Chapter 4: Celebrating Christ 107

    Sacrifice: The Pattern of Love 115

    The American Difficulty 119

    Festivity and an Authentic Humanity 125

    Conclusion 128

Conclusion 131

Introduction

There was a band director at my high school who, after hearing his band perform a difficult piece with technical precision, was nevertheless visibly frustrated by their performance. "Gentlemen," he said, "I need you to leave, fall in love with a girl, have her break your heart, and then come back and perform this piece." And then he dismissed the band. They did not lack skill or practice; what they lacked was humanity. They lacked what makes music, well, music.

There is perhaps no more pressing need in our time than to recover the wisdom of this band director. In an age of digital representation and manipulation, technical precision becomes the universal standard of quality, while the distinctly human element is brushed aside as something superfluous – a charming garnish to decorate an act, rather than the very thing that makes the act what it is. This band director knew that no matter how perfectly his students performed the music, if they themselves were not part of it, moving in and out of it as seamlessly as fish and water move in and out of each other, they were making rhythmic sounds, not performing music. Only one who has, in a sense, become the music he performs can express more than the mere musical notation on a page; only he can express the unspeakable mystery of which the written score is a mere symbol.

This reclaiming of the distinctly human element in life clearly extends beyond the realm of music. Indeed, it touches every dimension of life. What is the difference between a human being serving as a cashier at the grocery store and a machine? The cynic would tell us that the difference is that the machine works better than the cashier. But in doing so he reveals that for him, human beings are nothing more than inefficient machines. For him, the world is about utility and functionality. In such a world, there is no place for the infirm, for children, for love. Or rather, there is a place for them, but only inasmuch as they serve the real content of life, which is usefulness. That is what is really real. That is what matters. The human element is nice; certainly, nobody would want to get rid of it, but it is less important than the things that have to get done.

The same dynamic takes place within the realm of human knowing. What happens when someone knows something? Is it merely a matter of "downloading" information into his brain so that he can have easy access to it whenever it is needed? No, this is what a computer does. But perhaps human knowing means nothing more than computing, albeit less efficiently than the device we hold in our hands. Again, we are forced to ask the question: what, specifically, is the *human* element in human activity? And does that element even matter?

These are questions with which everyone must grapple, but it is above all necessary for the Christian, *the content of whose faith is the Person of Jesus Christ.*[2] In his work on faith, the German philosopher Josef Pieper offers a most provocative suggestion: "whoever undertakes to defend belief against the arguments of rationalism should prepare himself by considering the question: 'How do we apprehend a person?'"[3] Much like music communicates far more than musical notation in audible form, the Gospel communicates far more than mere information about God; it communicates the very Person of God in language adapted to the human mind. Whoever, then, wishes to promote the Gospel must do far more than creatively pass on information. No, his knowledge of the Gospel must so enter into his person that in communicating the Gospel, he is in fact communicating the One who dwells within him.

And if the Christian has a particular responsibility to grapple with the questions asked above, his task is made more difficult by the means by which Christ communicates himself to us: the sacramentality of his Body, the Church,

---

[2] Cf. Josef Pieper, "On Faith" in *Faith, Hope, Love*, trans. Richard and Clara Winston (San Francisco: Ignatius Press, 2012), 29-34.

[3] Ibid., 48.

effected by the ministry of the priest.[4] According to Pieper, it is the vocation of the priest to make present the Person of Jesus Christ in sacramental signs. He explains: "[the priest] is called, above all, to keep alive the remembrance of a face that our intuition just barely perceives behind all immediate and tangible reality – the face of the God-man, bearing the marks of a shameful execution."[5] Through sacramental signs, the priest makes visible the invisible Person who is present within all tangible reality.

And he must do so in an age that is ill-adapted to perceive persons through any signs at all. What we instinctually perceive when confronted with signs is not a person, but an idea. When someone receives a hand-written letter, he certainly receives the information communicated in it. But far more, he perceives the presence of a friend who is communicating that information. The anxiety of a hastily written note, the confidence of bold script, the insecurity of shaky hand-writing, all of these personal qualities are perceptible through the letter. And that personal presence is an essential part of the information itself. In a typed letter, however, that is obscured. It is too "heady." Even if one can perceive personal qualities

---

[4] Cf. John Paul II, *Ecclesia de Eucharistia* (Vatican City: Libreria Editrice Vaticana, 2003), 5-8.

[5] Josef Pieper, "Three Talks in a Sculptor's Studio" in *Only the Lover Sings: Art and Contemplation*, trans. Lothar Krauth (San Francisco: Ignatius Press, 1990), 62.

in the letter, he perceives them as something external to the letter, and not part of the letter itself. In other words, in our culture, signs no longer contain within themselves a personal presence, but a mere intellectual presence. We "know" there is a person on the other side of a typed letter, but that knowledge is more abstract, a mere idea, not something that is really experienced.

Sign and symbol, according to Pieper, are the very language of Christian faith.[6] We cannot know God if we do not "speak" sign. In a world that has largely forgotten how to speak this language, the Christian finds it difficult to encounter God's presence in the world. He approaches the sacraments (whether that be the seven individual sacraments or simply the sacramental nature of the Church) as he approaches an automated cashier: he looks for function, not for personal presence. If Christ communicates himself to us through sacramental signs, it is because He wants to offer us salvation through the gift of his very self, rather than through some external "fix." But only one capable of experiencing reality sacramentally will be able to receive his presence.

Pieper poses the crucial question: "How do we apprehend a person?" And while he does not explicitly answer this

---

[6] Josef Pieper, "Sign and Symbol as the Language of Christian Faith," in *Exercises in the Elements: Essays — Speeches — Notes*, trans. Daniel Farrelly (South Bend: St. Augustine's Press, 2019), 58-75.

question, his whole body of work invites the reader into a worldview that allows one to know a person. Many modern-day Christians know the content of the Christian faith within the existential framework of modernity, which is to say, they do not know the content of the Christian faith. By "existential framework of modernity," what I mean is this: no matter how Christian our theoretical concepts are, our living way of experiencing the world around us is one of utilitarian functionality. The Person of Jesus Christ is not that by which we experience the world; rather, we see the world by our modern standards, then try to add a Christian mentality onto that. This is why many find it difficult to *experience* the Gospel as good news, or sin as something detrimental to their being. Theoretically, we get it, but it does not seem to really affect us. What we need is a complete conversion, not thinking different things, but thinking differently. It is Pieper's great gift to the Church that his writings offer a Christian conceptual framework to those living in modern times. My hope through this work is to introduce to readers the worldview presented in Pieper's writings so that the Person of Jesus Christ may be made more accessible to their experience.

In order to preserve Pieper's gift of clarity in prose (even in translation!), I quote him extensively. Furthermore, rather than summarize his works, I sought to draw from as many of his works as possible in order to present his consistency of thought. Pieper has a unique ability to plunge disparate subject matters to their very depths and so show the unifying principal holding all reality together. Finally, given the emphasis on sharing Pieper's worldview such that readers may encounter Christ, this work is not of a scholarly nature, nor does it cite many of the excellent resources that further elucidate his thought for academic purposes. Instead, following Pieper's own style of writing, I have tried to present him in a manner as accessible as possible to any desiring to plunge into the depths of reality with him.

Finally, I offer a word on reading this book. Each chapter is introduced with a poem. For Pieper, poetry is expressive of the "divine madness" through which man, in the very loss of self-possession, finds a fulfillment he could not attain by his own power.[7] Humanity flourishes to the extent that man can be taken out of himself and his neatly explained world, and be brought into a world of which he is not in complete control. Such fulfillment requires a disposition of openness to the interruption of the divine into man's life. I begin each chapter with a poem in the hopes of fostering such openness in the course of one's reading. As much as rational thought is intended to give us a clear understanding of reality, even more, it is intended to *immerse us in* reality and thereby open our eyes to mystery. I wrote this book not primarily to

---

[7] Cf. Josef Pieper, *"Divine Madness": Plato's Case against Secular Humanism*, trans. Lothar Krauth (San Francisco: Ignatius Press, 1995), 7-8.

express ideas, but in the hope that the reader would become more capable of seeing the invisible through the visible in daily life. I ask, then, that anyone who reads this would do so in a contemplative spirit, allowing not only Pieper's or my voice to speak, but above all, God's Voice.

It is always a hopeless task to try to introduce others to a beloved author by using one's own words. If nothing else, my hope is that by reading this, readers will be inspired to pick up Pieper's works themselves and so be formed by this man to whom I am so indebted.

Chapter 1

Beholding Christ

"Transfiguration"

He led us up a Mountain,
His Voice awak'ning thrills of quiet hope,
And we, each step more frightened,
As were our hearts enlightened,
Beheld with awe the dizzying Summit's scope.

For surely by ascending
Would lose we all our stable sureties;
And with the slopes contending,
And all our might expending,
An end would come to trivialities.

More like the Mountain we
Became as though it hardened our resolve
To reach the Heights and see,
Inclined no more to flee;
Desire made our greatest fears dissolve.

At last we fixed our eyes
Upon the One who raised us from below;
We saw transfigured guise
As sight gave way to sighs;
Our Friend, his Glory he was pleased to show.

Now must we live in pain,
For vision's Joy remains upon the Height;
But we have been so changed,
That till we see again
That radiant Glory, find we no delight.

In the Easter Sequence, sung before the Gospel acclamation on Easter Sunday and throughout the Easter Octave, the Church recalls the wonder of the event of Christ's Resurrection. The sequence beautifully begins in the middle register, praising the Lord for reconciling sinners to the Father, then moves to the upper register to recount the wondrous combat waged between death and life in the Person of Jesus Christ. And then, suddenly, the hymn moves to the lower register, quietly and reverently asking Mary Magdalene a question: "Dic nobis Maria, quid vidisti in via?" "Tell us, Mary, what have you seen on the way?" In Mary's face, the Church recognizes *one who has seen* something and, in that vision, has found the fullness of life. And the Church longs to know what Mary has seen, the lower notes communicating the depth and intimacy of that longing.

"What have you seen?" For Pieper, the capacity to see is "that which actually constitutes man's vital existence, [which is] the perception of the reality of God and His creation, and the possibility of shaping himself and the world according to this truth, which reveals itself only in silence."[8] Man is fully himself only to the extent that he sees reality as it is and directs his life according to that vision. Pieper makes this point again and again. "The ultimate and genuine wealth of man –

---

[8] Josef Pieper, "Temperance" in *The Four Cardinal Virtues*, trans. Daniel F. Coogan (South Bend: Notre Dame Press, 2007), 202.

that which makes it worthwhile to be human – is his ability to grasp what is; his ability to be conscious of being itself and of things themselves not just as beneficial or harmful, useful or useless, but as being."⁹ "The perfectly happy person, the one whose thirst has finally been quenched, who has attained beatitude – this person is one who sees."¹⁰ Nearly every work of his in some way articulates the same statement: man is fully alive, fully himself, to the extent that he sees.

This conviction of Pieper's is by no means apparent to us. "What can be had on demand and almost gratis, and almost at once as well… necessarily loses both its value and its attractiveness."¹¹ Precisely because we have become capable of seeing so much whenever we want, we no longer recognize the value of seeing in our lives. We see things all the time and it hardly seems to give life. Indeed, at times it can seem to suck the life out of us. Everyone knows the experience of opening up one's email and immediately feeling anxious. We are aware of so much, and it is precisely this awareness, this "seeing," which is suffocating.

---

[9] Josef Pieper, "What does "Academic" mean?" in *What does "Academic" mean: Two Essays on the Chances of the University*, (South Bend: St. Augustine's Press, 2015), 26.

[10] Josef Pieper, *Happiness and Contemplation*, trans. Richard and Clara Winston (South Bend: St. Augustine's Press, 1998), 58.

[11] Josef Pieper, "On Love" in *Faith, Hope, Love*, trans. Richard and Clara Winston, 266.

Apparently, there is seeing and there is seeing. Not all seeing is alike. "There are levels and grades, which go from fleeting awareness, to rational thinking, to intellectual sight and vision."[12] And while each level has its proper place, only the last constitutes that form of seeing that makes man fully alive and integrates the other levels of perception into a fully human life. And yet, it is precisely this form of seeing that has all but disappeared from day-to-day life, so much so that it has really become a foreign concept.

Having a "fleeting awareness" of something is abundantly familiar, as we are surrounded by all sorts of sensory stimuli. And most of us are wondering how to "turn off" our capacity for rational thinking since everything we experience is presented to us as an object of analysis (including, and perhaps especially, ourselves). We incessantly examine the world and ourselves hoping to make new discoveries for the sake of having more control, and we find it exhausting. But simple intellectual sight and vision? This, we must admit, is no longer readily understood. "Man's ability to *see* is in decline...." says Pieper, "because *there is too much to see.*"[13]

---

[12] Josef Pieper, "What Does Happiness Mean? Fulfillment in Vision" in *Exercises in the Elements: Essays – Speeches – Notes*, trans. Daniel Farrelly (South Bend: St. Augustine's Press, 2019), 127.

[13] Pieper, "Learning How to See Again" in *Only the Lover Sings*, 31-32.

Contemplation and Wonder

This statement of Pieper's is a helpful starting point for us to comprehend what he means by "intellectual sight and vision." He encourages a certain "asceticism of cognition" as a means of preserving our fundamental capacity to see reality as it is. Such encouragement is by no means a flight into ignorance, driven by fear of scientific knowledge.[14] Nor is it driven by an excessive gravitas that does not allow for the incorporation of trivial happenings into a fully human life. It is, rather, an encouragement to properly consider the place of scientific knowledge and of trivialities in the whole of human life. The person who fills his life solely with these forms of seeing does not see too much, but too little of reality. He loses the capacity to see the *mirandum* of being, the wonder of all reality.[15]

For Pieper, to see reality as it is, one must recognize that it is simultaneously knowable and unfathomable, which is to say, one must recognize the creaturely nature of our knowing.[16] Everything that exists that is not God, exists as *creatura*.

---

[14] Cf. Pieper, "The Problem of Faith Today" in *Problems of Modern Faith: Essays and Addresses*, trans. Jan van Huerck (Chicago: Franciscan Herald Press, 1985), 1-11.

[15] Cf. *Happiness and Contemplation*, 75 and *What Does "Academic" mean?*, 26.

[16] Much of this paragraph (as well as some other sections of this chapter) is drawn from my dissertation, "Rejoicing in

This means that when we are looking at something, we are looking at an object whose being has already been determined by another's mind. If I look at the *Mona Lisa* and I say that it is a donkey, I am wrong. But I can be wrong only because what the *Mona Lisa* "is" has already been determined by Leonardo da Vinci. The *Mona Lisa* has *received* its "whatness" from da Vinci. But it *gives* its "whatness" to everyone else. All who look upon this work of art are able to know it only because it is first known by the artist. Likewise, when we look upon anything in the world, we are looking upon objects which have received their essence from the Divine Mind. In creating, God forms reality according to the idea He has in his mind. And only because of his *prior* knowledge are we able to have knowledge of creation at all.[17]

But that which makes creation knowable is the same as that which makes it unfathomable. "God forms creation according to the idea He has in his mind." That "idea" is nothing other than God Himself. The doctrine of creation states that God has formed all that is *ex nihilo*. This means that in creating, God has no model to base his creation on other than

---

Creation: Josef Pieper's Response to a World of Online Distractions" (STD diss., The Catholic University of America, 2020), 67-70).

[17] Cf. Pieper, "The Truth of All Things" in *Living the Truth*, trans. Lothar Krauth (San Francisco: Ignatius Press, 1989), 52-53 (emphasis in the original).

Himself. All of creation, then, is a created participation in the Uncreated Essence of God. To fully know what something is, to truly see it in its entirety, would mean to see the Infinite God. The same light that allows us to know anything at all is also a blinding light. Pieper explains:

> ...the inscrutability of things is almost the same as their knowability. This common root... is the *createdness* of things, i.e., the truth that the designs, the archetypal patterns of things, dwell within the Divine Logos. Because things come forth from the eye of God, they partake wholly of the nature of the Logos, that is, they are lucid and limpid to their very depths. It is their origin in the Logos which makes them knowable to men. But because of this very origin in the Logos, they mirror an *infinite* light and can therefore not be wholly comprehended. It is not darkness or chaos which makes them unfathomable. If a man, therefore... gropes after the essence of things, he finds himself, by the very act of approaching his object, in an unfathomable abyss, but it is an abyss of *light*.[18]

---

[18] Josef Pieper, "The Timeliness of Thomism" in *The Silence of St. Thomas: Three Essays*, trans. John Murray, S.J. and Daniel O'Connor (Chicago: Henry Regnery Co., 1965), 96.

When anyone truly sees anything, his experience is simultaneously one of knowledge and of wonder. On the one hand, he knows what he sees. On the other hand, he knows it as so far surpassing his knowledge.

Thus, when Pieper encourages an asceticism of cognition, he does so with a view to preserving man's capacity to see God in the world. In our attempt to see everything, to make everything transparent to our vision, there is a dangerous pride that reduces creation to a mere artifact, to what can be wholly and expediently comprehended. But in doing so, we no longer experience the joy of encountering the Infinite through the finite. And it is this, Pieper argues, that brings us fulness of life: "the ultimate fulfillment, the absolutely meaningful activity, the most perfect expression of being alive, the deepest satisfaction, and the fullest achievement of human existence must needs happen in an instance of beholding, namely in the contemplating awareness of the world's ultimate and intrinsic foundations."[19] Only when we see the Infinite Logos are we truly fulfilled; and only in the light of this vision do we also properly see the created world.

---

[19] Josef Pieper, "Work, Spare Time, and Leisure" in *Only the Lover Sings*, 22.

Contemplation of God in Human Misery

The temptation to reduce the whole of creation to a mere artifact, however, is very real. According to Pieper, the challenge of contemplation is two-fold. First:

> Anyone who considers the evil in this world with an uncorrupted eye and sincere concern may... possibly say: How can we praise contemplation of this earthly creation when the ages, the present age and probably all ages, have been full of disorder, frightful injustice, hunger, painful deaths, oppression and every form of human misery? Is it possible to keep in mind the actual history of mankind and at the same time speak of the happiness of intuition, of satiation and beatitude? Is this anything but flight from the real world, an attempt to render horrors innocuous, a form of self-deception and unrealistic idyllicism? Ought not a generous person who does not care to deceive himself about what is going on in the world day after day – ought not such a person have the courage to renounce the "escape" of happiness?[20]

Such a challenge cannot be easily set aside. If we find happiness and fulfillment by beholding "the world's ultimate and

---

[20] Pieper, *Happiness and Contemplation*, 105.

intrinsic foundations," it is well worth asking whether such foundation truly exists. Is the world, in spite of all appearances, fundamentally meaningful?

If the answer to this question is "no," then there can be no doubt that the desire for contemplation is vain. In such a case, one ought not waste his time hoping to "see" the meaning of the world, but rather should try, as best as he can, to *give* the world meaning by his own efforts. The responsible thing, it seems, is to see the world, not as *creatura*, but as "simply the arena, the stuff, the raw material of human activity."[21] In short, to reduce creation to an artifact. By rejecting the inherent meaningfulness of reality, the world ceases to be something worthy of beholding and becomes, instead, something in need of fixing. And the more power and control we exercise over the world, the more meaning we are able to infuse into it and so rid the world of its brokenness.

This, Pieper argues, is the world in which we find ourselves. We look at the world not as *creatura*, but as dead matter:

> The world in which man today leads his ordinary life is becoming more and more a purely technological

---

[21] Josef Pieper, "What Does It Mean to Philosophize?" In *For the Love of Wisdom: Essays on the Nature of Philosophy*, ed. Berthold Wald, trans. Roger Wasserman (San Francisco: Ignatius Press, 2006), 39.

one. The things with which he is concerned are artificial; they are artifacts, not creations. The danger inherent in this situation is that man might, erroneously, come to regard the world as a whole and the created things with it — above all, man himself — in the same manner in which he regards, correctly, his own artifacts belonging to the technological sphere; in other words, man is beginning to consider the whole of creation as completely fathomable, fully accessible to rational comprehension, and, above all, as something which it is permissible to change, transform, or even destroy.[22]

More and more, we look to technology to solve the problem of human misery. The experience of brokenness in the world alerts us to the fundamental meaninglessness of reality, it seems, and the more we can fix the world's brokenness, the more we can fix the problem of the world's meaninglessness. We need only exert more power and control. In such a world, there is no place for a contemplative "beholding" of reality, but only of a thinking about reality that will bear fruit in the practical betterment of our lives.

Pieper, however, argues that even the brokenness of the world has become incorporated into our contemplating awareness of the world's ultimate and intrinsic foundations.

---

[22] Josef Pieper, "The Timeliness of Thomism," 91-92.

The world's brokenness does not call the meaningfulness of reality into question; rather, it becomes the very place where the world's meaning is revealed. "Earthly contemplation," Pieper says, "means to the Christian… this above all: that behind all that we directly encounter the Face of the incarnate Logos becomes visible.… [But] the Face of the Divine Man bears the marks of a shameful execution."[23] The vision that is offered in contemplation does not ignore the historical reality of human misery. But that misery serves to reveal the meaning of the world, which is communion with God. The world is meaningful because it is known to its very depths by the Logos; indeed, known even in its misery.

Consequently, Pieper declares, "the happiness of contemplation is a true happiness, indeed the supreme happiness, but it is founded upon sorrow."[24] To see the Infinite through the finite, one must be able to see, at least in some form, the God who was crucified and rose again, still bearing the marks of his crucifixion. The full depth of this will only be seen after we examine the second challenge that Pieper presents to our contemplative awareness of reality.

---

[23] Josef Pieper, *Happiness and Contemplation*, 108.
[24] Ibid.

Contemplation and Transcendence of Self

The second challenge of contemplation, which tempts us to reduce the world to a mere artifact, is the discomfiting experience it brings of being shaken out of our "neatly explained world."[25] Because what one sees in contemplation cannot be comprehended, the vision awakens an insatiable longing. To know something means, ultimately, to *be* that which one knows. There is no more intimate union than that which exists between knower and known. So, if in contemplation we come to know that which transcends our knowledge, this means that we *become* that which transcends our nature. This requires a somewhat technical understanding of the nature of intellectual knowledge, but it is a study that is at once illuminating and disquieting.

Pieper, following St. Thomas and Aristotle, argues that knowing something means knowing the thing's "form," knowing that which makes it what it is. A thing is what it is because it has a definite form. Wine is wine because it has the form of "wine-ness." But the person who knows wine as wine *also* has the form of wine-ness. But to have a form means to be that thing since it is the form that makes something what

---

[25] Josef Pieper, *"Divine Madness": Plato's Case against Secular Humanism*, trans. Lothar Krauth (San Francisco: Ignatius Press, 1995), 42.

it is. Thus, the person who knows wine is, in an intelligible sense, wine. Pieper explains:

> For a thing to have knowledge, then, means to carry in itself the identity (*quidditas*) of some other being or thing, and not only its "image" but indeed its "form." A being's ability to know, therefore, is its ability to transcend its own delimitations, the ability to step out of its own identity and to have "also the form of the other being," which means: to *be* the other being. "Knowing" constitutes and establishes the most intimate relationship conceivable between two beings (a fact that is expressed and confirmed in the age-old usage of "knowing" to indicate sexual intercourse).[26]

For this reason, Aristotle argued that the soul is, in a sense, all things since its ability to know reaches to the whole universe of being.

This may seem like a good bit of philosophical mumbo-jumbo, but it is helpful to consider that Pieper is intending to explain an experience that is not wholly foreign to us. At what point can someone truly say that he "knows" another? When he has enough details of the other's life? No. We all know that true knowledge requires more than that. To truly

---

[26] Pieper, "The Truth of All Things," 37.

"know" another, we must participate in the other's life. "The mind perceives a thing by way of participation in the other's intrinsic nature, and this participation is conceived... as a relationship of actual identity between mind and objective reality."[27] Only when the two become one can we really say that we know what we know.

But this requires a never-ending immersion in the intrinsic nature of the known object. In *Boys in the Boat*, which tells the story of the American 1936 Olympic crew team, the author places before us the renowned George Pocock. Pocock spent his life crafting racing shells, and his expertise won him universal acclamation. But the author shows us a man who simply loved the craft of boat-making. Pocock *knew* these boats. He knew which trees would provide the best wood for the boats to move fast in certain conditions. He knew how the wood would bend when it interacted with water. Through a life-long relationship with these boats (and the trees he used to make them), Pocock himself was formed *by* them, even as he formed them. He did not materially become the boats he made, but in some way he was in them, and they were in him. It would be impossible to understand this man if one did not also understand the boats he made.

Now, racing shells are not made of wood. They are manufactured in factories and made of "synthetics such as fiber-

---

[27] Ibid., 38.

glass and carbon-fiber composites."[28] They can be built faster, with greater consistency, and they move more quickly in the water. But the manufacturers do not *know* the boats in the same way that Pocock did. Indeed, they cannot. They are too remote to really be affected by the boats they make. They themselves are not *in* the boats in the same way; nor are the boats *in* them. Efficiency and productivity? Yes. But intimacy and identity? No.

To know something in the way that Pieper is talking about requires that one immerse himself in a life-long pursuit of intimacy with what is known. And in that pursuit, he becomes more and more aware of the beauty of that which he sees, and he knows that it is forever beyond his grasp. He realizes that the tangible reality presented to his senses is only a gateway to an intangible mystery to which he longs to be united. And so the pursuit is endless, yet not hopeless. His knowledge leads him to continually transcend himself until he is transformed into the very mystery that he beholds.

Because this process of knowing is painful and difficult, and requires a renunciation of one's self-enclosed world, we pull back from such an encounter with the ineffability of creation. We reduce creation to an artifact so that we can be comfortably grounded within the confines our own minds. The problem is *not* that we treat the things we encounter in

---

[28] Daniel Brown, *Boys in the Boat* (New York: Penguin Books, 2014), 364.

this world as artifacts. Doing so belongs to our dignity as co-creators along with the Creator. Indeed, George Pocock is a magnificent example of one who transformed trees into boats by the careful process of measuring and calculating. That is not the problem. The danger comes when we have so much mastery and understanding over creation that we forget it is creation; that we come to consider, as Pieper says, "the whole of creation as completely fathomable, fully accessible to rational comprehension, and, above all, as something which it is permissible to change, transform, or even destroy."

Such reflections may seem overly "mystical," but that only reveals how comfortable we have become in an isolated world that is overly concerned with efficiency and productivity. And this is not merely the effect of modernity, but is the effect of sin, of seeking to remove God from the world. Pieper's understanding of the real capacity of human knowing to unite us to what is known should make us pause. How well do we really know anything? Might not the prevalence of man's feeling of isolation in the world be traced back to a willed decision to close our eyes to anything other than what can be fully grasped? By shielding ourselves from the disquieting experience of contemplation, we have shielded ourselves also from fullness of life – from being drawn into communion with that which holds all reality in existence.

This insight from Pieper is drawn from a traditional "distinction between two types of knowledge: between genuinely theoretical knowledge, knowledge *per cognitionem*, and knowledge that occurs on the basis of a community of nature, knowledge *per connaturalitatem*..."[29] It is worth quoting Pieper at length, since his words have an immediate relevance for the contemplative awareness of God in the world:

> In the first case, the object of knowledge is something foreign; in the second case, what is known is something belonging to oneself. In the case of the first kind of knowledge, a moralist or ethicist, for example, who need not be a good person himself, determines what is good; in the case of the second type of knowledge, knowledge *per connaturalitatem*, the good person recognizes what is good – on the basis of his immediate participation and involvement, on the basis of an inner attunement, thanks to the unerring instincts of the lover (for love is that through which the alien becomes one's own, that through which the *connaturalitatem* arises – as Aquinas also notes). Only someone who, to use an expression of Dionysius the Areopagite, is not only "learned in the divine but also experienced in the sufferance of it" can preside over divine things as if they were his own due to a shared community of nature.[30]

---

[29] Pieper, "What Does It Mean to Philosophize?" 80.
[30] Ibid.

If one is to see the divine ground of all being, it is not enough for him to know about it through study, keeping it at a distance in safe observation. Rather, he must know it through his own sharing in the divine nature.

This is possible, however, because the divine nature has *first* known human nature to its very depths. When Pieper argues that the world is fundamentally meaningful because known by God, he means that God is in his creation. Certainly, He is not present in a pantheistic way, as if all creation is God Himself.[31] But nevertheless, in *all* creation dwells the active and abiding presence of God. For the creature, to "be" means to "be in relation to God." This is so much the case that "there is no need for 'something' to happen for the creature to sink back into the nothingness from which it springs; literally 'nothing' needs to happen for this sinking back to come about, all that is required is for creation to cease happening."[32]

This is the case *even in the historical reality of human misery*. This is why Pieper can argue with such conviction that

---

[31] Cf. Josef Pieper, *No One Could Have Known: An Autobiography: The Early Years, 1904-1945*, trans. Graham Harrison (San Francisco: Ignatius Press, 1987), 106-107. Interestingly, the book-form of Pieper's dissertation was cautiously denied an imprimatur for fear of a (incorrect) pantheist reading.

[32] Josef Pieper, *The End of Time: A Meditation on the Philosophy of History*, trans. Michael Bullock (San Francisco: Ignatius Press, 1999), 62-63.

the world is fundamentally meaningful even in the midst of the world's horrors. In seeing "the face of the God-man, bearing the marks of a shameful execution," we behold the act of God's knowing the world to its very depths. He takes on the form of broken humanity, which means He becomes broken humanity. And because He takes on this form without ceasing to be God, and with no change in the divine nature occurring, human nature becomes capable of participating in the divine nature. In short, man is able to see God because he has first been seen by Him.

If man barricades himself against his experiences of suffering, he loses his capacity to see God. He looks for meaning in something other than the presence of the Divine Logos permeating all creation. Only by accepting the challenges inherent in contemplation can man become fully himself by beholding the divine ground of all being.

The Contemplative Christian

When Mary Magdalen saw the Risen Lord, her vision was neither the result of physical seeing nor of careful study, but of intimate sharing in his life. She was present at his crucifixion, when He had known her brokenness to its depths. And she stayed with Him in that brokenness. She let herself be known. And precisely because He knew her brokenness, that same brokenness ceased to have power over her. All that calls the meaningfulness of the world into question was flipped on its head at the crucifixion. This is what Mary has seen, as stated in the Easter Sequence: "Sepulchrum Christi viventis, et gloriam vidi resurgentis." "I have seen the sepulchre of the living Christ, and the glory of the risen one." She saw these, not by her eyesight, but by the union of her intimate knowledge of the Lord.

The Christian life is necessarily contemplative. The Christian is first and foremost a witness – one who has seen something. And what he has seen is the life of the risen Lord, perceived by his own experience of new life. He is experienced in the sufferance of the divine; he allows God to draw close to his own brokenness. Only in this way can salvation, which is fullness of life, be truly communicated to him, since it consists in nothing other than the "existential attunement... with the divine ground of being, without which we know ourselves to be lost along with all that is best in us."[33]

What this attunement looks like, and how it is brought about, will be the content of the rest of this little book. This chapter is given to contextualize Pieper's relevance for the Christian. Only if we understand what it means to "see" God can we appreciate the import of the sacraments, administered by the priest, "who is called, above all, to keep alive the remembrance of a face that our intuition just barely perceives

---

[33] Pieper, *The Concept of Sin*, trans. Edward T. Oakes (South Bend: St. Augustine's Press, 2001), 52.

behind all immediate and tangible reality – the face of the God-man, bearing the marks of a shameful execution."

Chapter 2

Becoming Christ

"Photina"

From highest mountains, springs of living water
Flow forth with gleeful sounds of rushing ardor,
    Drawing all people who in languor wither
        Up to its high Source.

Parched for fulfillment, thirsting, man seeks endless
    Joys and an ever-lasting Home for comfort;
        Yet in this finite world of sullied waters
            Often thirst wanders.

Still nothing hinders those pure waters streaming.
    In haste they plummet to the caverns deepest,
        To sate a longing whose thirst goes yet deeper
           Than one can fathom.

Drawn by this longing for fulfillment's waters,
Thirst climbs the mountain to rejoin its own source;
    All pow'rs uniting in harmonious movement,
        Ever ascending.

The shift from being "someone who skis" to a "skier" is rather imperceptible. One who is learning to ski finds himself fighting against the movement of the mountain. Everything in him and around him is pushing him downwards, and he is trying to prevent that from happening. Or at least, he wants to control the manner of this downward plunge. He looks clumsy, out of place on the mountain, and his experience of skiing is exhausting. The skier, by contrast, moves in harmony with the mountain's plummeting slopes. He no longer fights the mountain's gravitational pull as if it were his mortal enemy. Rather, he embraces it as the very means by which he will arrive at his destination. His body, having learned the mountain's movements, is able to act in accord with them. He dives down the mountain effortlessly and joyfully, at home in the mountain's world.

So, it is with one who is attuned to the divine ground of being. There is a movement within man, a gravitational pull, so to speak, directing him to the *bonum universale* – to "goodness so very good that there is nothing in it which is not good, and nothing outside of it which could be good."[34] Man longs to become fully himself by taking into himself "the whole good," which "taking in" happens by means of beholding that good. And everything in man moves him in the direction of taking in the good. Every desire, every hope, points in some way to the fulfillment of man's nature.

---

[34] Pieper, *Happiness and Contemplation*, 40

We act, however, like "someone who lives," rather than a "liver," so to speak. We find ourselves moving against the gravitational pull of being, trying to control the manner of our desiring. And for good reason: like the mountain's gravitational force, man's gravitational pull towards the good has the potential of disastrous consequences. We are right to reverence the power of our desires and, to a certain extent, to fear them. It would be reckless and immature to assume every movement of our desire will bring us to our destination of union with the good, of fullness of life.

But this fear can also lead us to reject our creaturely nature, to seek such control over our movement towards fulfillment that we no longer trust that the movement is good at all. The effect of this is that we no longer readily understand what the Christian tradition means by "virtue":

> The Middle Ages also said something about virtue that is no longer readily understood – least of all by Kant's compatriots and disciples – they held that virtue meant: "mastering our natural bent." No; that is what Kant would have said, and we all of us find it quite easy to understand; what Aquinas says is that virtue makes us perfect by enabling us to *follow* our natural bent in the right way.[35]

---

[35] Josef Pieper, *Leisure, the Basis of Culture*, trans. Alexander Dru (San Francisco: Ignatius Press, 2009), 33-34.

The ease with which we misunderstand virtue indicates how far we have come along the path of self-rejection. We assume the desires and movements of our hearts for fulfillment are bad (or at least irrational), and we seek to master them. But by so suspecting our created nature, we cease to trust the creative presence of the Creator within us. We do not listen to the melody playing within our own nature, and so we cannot live in harmony with it, try as we might to live morally upright lives.

Instead, Pieper invites us to live in "existential attunement" to the divine ground of being by expressing in our lives a deep affirmation of God's creation (including that creation which is ourselves). The voice emanating within us that calls us to self-fulfillment expresses "a total affirmation of the meaning of the world… [and] the ethical necessity of man's conscious self-coordination with the direction of the movement of total reality."[36] Man's great "yes!" to creation and his fullest expression of the divine life within him is manifest in a life of virtue. As St. Irenaeus says: "the glory of God is man fully alive." God is made manifest in the flesh of one who lives in accord with the truth of his being.

In Pieper's language, this simply means that the virtuous life is the life of a man in love. The first and principle

---

[36] Josef Pieper, "Reality and the Good" in *Living the Truth*, 160. Cf. also, "Contemporary Relevance of the Cardinal Virtues" in *Exercises in the Elements: Essays – Speeches – Notes*, 102-103.

movement of love, he says, is the affirmation of being. Love proclaims: "It's good that you are; how wonderful that you exist!"[37] It is the echo in our hearts of that first proclamation: "Let there be..." The man who lives in love, lives in accord with reality. What Pieper offers us, then, is an articulation of what happens in a man when all that is in him affirms the gravitational pull of his nature towards fulfillment in God, who is the *bonum universale*. And while it is beyond the scope of this work to examine in depth each of Pieper's works on the theological and cardinal virtues, we can see, in outline fashion, what it looks like for man to be fully alive.

The Christian Idea of Man

Before examining Pieper's articulation of the fully human life, it is worth pausing to consider the courage and magnanimity needed to live a life of virtue. On the one hand, the man who undertakes the challenge to live a virtuous life accepts the arduous task of directing his mind, his will, and his appetites according to "the movement of total reality." He accepts the task of knowing reality as it is (and not as he would like it to be), and of conforming his life to that truth. This endeavor requires a total commitment of self: "a tremendous activity of the will is required if we are to be determined only by reality in our knowing, to be objective and to force

---

[37] Pieper, "On Love" in *Faith, Hope, Love*, 170.

ourselves to silence and to keep ourselves out of the picture and so to become perceptive."[38] To commit to a life of virtue means to be willing to submit all one's hopes and desires to the judgment of truth.

On the other hand, however, a life of virtue consists in living according to the truth *as it is known by the individual himself*. Only the individual himself can determine what is the most fitting means of accomplishing the good in the concrete circumstances of his life.[39] This is not to say that there are no moral decisions that are universally applicable for all time: "the goals of human action do not change, nor do man's basic directions. For every 'condition' of man, at all times and

---

[38] Pieper, "Reality and the Good," 135.

[39] Josef Pieper, "Prudence" in *The Four Cardinal* Virtues, trans. Richard and Clara Winston, 28-29. It should be noted that there is one exception to this: "A friend, and a *prudent* friend, can help to shape a friend's decision. He does so by virtue of that love which makes the friend's problem his own, the friend's ego his own… For by virtue of that oneness which love can establish he is able to visualize it from, as it were, the actual center of responsibility. Therefore it is possible for a friend – only for a friend and only for a *prudent* friend – to help with counsel and direction to shape a friend's decision or, somewhat in the manner of a judge, help to reshape it. Such genuine and prudent loving friendship (*amor amicitiae*) – which has nothing in common with sentimental intimacy, and indeed is rather imperiled by such intimacy – is the *sine qua non* for genuine spiritual guidance. For only this empowers another to offer the kind of direction which – almost! – conforms to the concrete situation in which the decision must be made."

places, he is under the obligation to be just and brave and temperate."[40] This is especially true in the realm of justice, which "are most independent of changes in situations and are therefore most likely to be fixed once and for all."[41] Nevertheless, it is the individual himself who must hold himself responsible for his actions, for living in accord with reality as he has come to know it. He cannot offload that responsibility onto a pre-determined set of rules that have been elaborately developed by professional moralists.

This was the approach developed in the casuist tradition. Recognizing the need for clarity in challenging moral cases, teachers of moral theology sought to determine the morality of particular acts as an aid to confessors, in particular. And as an aid, this form of teaching certainly has merit. But, according to Pieper, "[a] moral theology that relies too much upon casuistry necessarily becomes a 'science of sins' instead of a doctrine of virtues, or a theory of the Christian idea of man."[42] Rather than looking at what it means to be human, such a moral theology looks instead at what is "allowed" and especially at what is "not allowed."[43] The creative dynamism of the human drive towards the good is stifled by the fear of doing something prohibited. Pieper continues: "[a] merely

---

[40] Ibid., 25.

[41] Ibid., 26.

[42] Ibid., 30.

[43] Cf. Josef Pieper, *The Christian Idea of Man*, trans. Dan Farrelly (South Bend: St. Augustine's Press, 2011), 4.

casuistic moral theology assumes the immaturity of human beings. Moreover, it intensifies and perpetuates this immaturity."[44] When morality is reduced to a list of what is permitted or not, the grandeur of man's capacity to live the truth recedes to the background as a moralistic system comes to the fore.

Herein lies the magnanimity of the virtuous man. He simultaneously submits to the primacy of truth and reality, while upholding also his own responsibility to live in accord with that truth according to the unique circumstances of his life and the various characteristics of his personality. The virtuous man does not conform to a system, but to truth. Even in acts of justice, which allow for the least variation of change, it still matters *who it is* that is performing that act of justice. The person's own appropriation of truth never becomes irrelevant. He, and he alone, can perform this particular act. No other person will ever perform that act of justice again: "…the specific ways of accomplishing [the] unchanging obligation [to be just and brave and temperate] may take a thousand different forms."[45] There are as many ways to be virtuous as there are persons in the world. And because only persons can perform virtuous acts, a virtuous life manifests the infinite goodness of God, which cannot be expressed in any once-and-for-all system.

---

[44] Pieper, "Prudence," 31.
[45] Ibid.

Because of the value given to efficiency and security in our lives, the casuist tradition has a certain appeal to us. In many of our day-to-day tasks, we offload responsibility onto systems that ensure for us a positive outcome for certain tasks. These are certainly indispensable tools for living in modern culture. But they can also dispose us to reject the magnanimous call to a virtuous life, and to prefer, instead, a life concerned with not breaking the rules. As we build cars that have more and more self-driving features, we forget that it is *we* who are driving the car. In some ways, the car may work better, but the person certainly does not. So many of our everyday tasks dispose us to forget that *we* are the principal agents of our actions. The effect of this on our moral lives is a diminished emphasis on our existential attunement to reality and an exaggerated emphasis on rules. Whether the response to that is a neurotic following of rules or a rebellious rejection of them, the *person* is lost behind the *actions*.

Clearly, the point in this is not to revert to an immature form of moral anarchy, but rather to reclaim the personal dimension of Christian morality. For Pieper, "…moral teaching is first and foremost teaching about man; [it] must make the idea of man visible; and… therefore Christian moral teaching must deal with a Christian exemplar of man."[46] And this means looking towards a person, rather than a system. Again, Pieper makes the central point: "The answer to the question

---

[46] Josef Pieper, *The Christian Idea of Man*, 3

about the Christian exemplar for man can be given in a single sentence. It can be expressed exhaustively in a single word: Christ. The Christian ought to be 'another Christ'..."[47] The moral "system" thus chosen by the Christian tradition that preserves the personal call to union with Christ, while also giving concrete expression to that union, is a morality of virtue.

Pieper follows Thomas Aquinas:

Thomas Aquinas, the great master of Western Christendom, decided to express the Christian idea of man in seven theses: First, the Christian is a person who, in his *faith*, is aware of the reality of the Trinity. Second, the Christian looks forward – in *hope* – to the ultimate fulfillment of his being in eternal life. Third, the Christian – with the Theological Virtue of *love* – turns to God and his fellow man, affirming them with a love that is far stronger than any natural love. Fourth, the Christian is prudent, i.e. he does not let his view of reality be clouded by what the will dictates without reference to the truth about the real situation. Fifth, the Christian is just, i.e. he is able to live the truth "with the other"; he sees that he is one member among other members of the Church, of the population, and of the all-embracing community. Sixth,

---

[47] Ibid., 5.

the Christian is brave, i.e. he is prepared to be harmed – and even to accept death, if necessary – for truth and for the realization of justice. Seventh, the Christian is moderate, i.e. he does not allow his desire for possessions and enjoyment to become destructive and repugnant to his being.[48]

This sevenfold schema of the virtues prevents the Christian idea of man from falling into an abstraction and generalization, on the one hand, and into a set of rules and prohibitions, on the other hand. By expressing the Christian idea of man according to the virtues, we are able to see and articulate God's life in man – a life that is at once visible and mysterious.

Prudence

In writing his books about the virtues, Pieper did not set out to develop an ahistorical schema of them, as did St. Thomas Aquinas. His writing was historically conditioned, for example, writing his first work on the virtue of fortitude as a correction to the Nazi propaganda about the courageous man. He draws from the wisdom of tradition to show the contemporary relevance of the doctrine of virtue.

Nevertheless, again and again, he emphasizes the importance of a metaphysical hierarchy of the virtues. There is

---

[48]Ibid., 6-7.

an order: first, prudence, then justice, fortitude, and finally temperance. We are wont to smile at such seemingly inane hierarchical ordering. But for Pieper, the ordering of the virtues itself reveals the truth of who man is. Indeed, he argues:

> [N]othing less than the whole ordered structure of the Occidental Christian view of man rests upon the pre-eminence of prudence over the other virtues. The structural framework of Occidental Christian metaphysics as a whole stands revealed, perhaps more plainly than in any other single ethical dictum, in the proposition that prudence is the foremost of the virtues. That structure is built thus: that Being precedes Truth, and that Truth precedes the Good. Indeed, the living fire at the heart of the dictum is the central mystery of Christian theology: that the Father begets the Eternal Word, and that the Holy Spirit proceeds out of the Father and the Word.[49]

That prudence is the first and "mother" of all virtues is the necessary ethical expression of man's being made in the image and likeness of God. To lose sight of this hierarchy and to consign it to a realm of unimportance is to lose sight of the Christian understanding of man's dignity originating from his being made in God's image.

---

[49] Pieper, "Prudence," 3-4.

Prudence is the first and "mother" of all virtues. It is her role to transform the purely receptive knowledge of reality into the creative knowledge which forms good action. Through prudence, man's reason rightly *beholds* the good to be done (that which is in accord with reality) and then *commands* that good to be accomplished in man's concrete life. Thus, whenever we see a just act being performed, we are seeing the embodied expression of what the just man has seen in his mind's eye. As St. Theophilus of Antioch says, "If you say to me, 'Show me your God,' I will say to you, 'show me what kind of person you are, and I will show you my God.' Show me then whether the eyes of your mind can see, and the ears of your heart hear."[50] What the mind has seen, what "God" man has known, becomes visible and incarnate only through the virtue of prudence.

But because man can only behold the invisible through the visible, and the general through the particular, it belongs to prudence to deal with the particulars of human action. Man does not know his final end – which is God – through prudence but through faith. By submitting his intellect to the truth which he does not see, but which he believes because of the attractiveness of the One who has seen, man

---

[50] Theophilus of Antioch, "From the book addressed to Autolycus by Saint Theophilus of Antioch, bishop" in *The Liturgy of the Hours, Vol. II* (New York: Catholic Book Publishing Corp., 1976), 240.

participates in the same knowledge as the One who sees. By faith, man knows the Infinite Fulfillment available to him in God and directs himself towards that end. But the life of faith only becomes "real" for him through the virtue of prudence, by which he knows the means towards the end which is given him by faith.

But there is a nearly infinite number of means by which man can act justly, bravely, and temperately. It belongs to prudence to determine the most fitting means of doing so in concrete circumstances. Hence, prudence relies for its realization on a number of other intellectual virtues: true-to-being memory, by which man rightly remembers experiences so that he may judge future principles of action in truth;[51] docility, by which he recognizes his own need for other's assistance and experiences in forming his mind;[52] *solertia*, by which "man, when confronted with a sudden event, does not close his eyes by reflex and then blindly... take action. Rather... he can swiftly, but with open eyes and clear-sighted vision, decide for the good;"[53] and foresight, by which "is meant the capacity to estimate, with a sure instinct for the future, whether a particular action will lead to the realization

---

[51] Cf. Ibid., 14-15.
[52] Cf. Ibid., 16.
[53] Ibid.

of the goal."⁵⁴ Without such aids, man cannot hope to choose rightly the means to accomplish the good to be done.

Yet even with these aids, it does not belong to man to have absolute certainty of the correctness of his action. Pieper quotes Aquinas: "the certitude of prudence cannot be so great as completely to remove all anxiety." He continues: "Man, then, when he comes to a decision, cannot ever be sufficiently prescient nor can he wait until logic affords him absolute certainty."⁵⁵ Here we see again how opposed the life of virtue is to a life of efficiency which strives to remove all malfunctioning and errors. In human action, there is *always* lack of certainty. Man can never escape the peril of being man (except, perhaps, by barricading himself by fear in a world of false-certainties).

Yet at the same time, man can approach greater certitude by means of growth in charity and the grace of the Holy Spirit. As man grows in friendship with God, he sees reality more and more with the unfailing instincts of a lover. He has a "taste" for the good, which allows him, even when he cannot articulate it, to know what is the good to be accomplished. Furthermore, God Himself acts upon the human mind by the Holy Spirit's gift of counsel, which, indeed,

---

⁵⁴ Ibid., 18. Here it becomes clear that Pieper is not giving a systematic exposition of the virtues, as he leaves out other "quasi-integral parts" of prudence given by St. Thomas, namely, understanding, reason, circumspection, and caution.

⁵⁵ Ibid.

opens up an even greater realm of possibilities for action. We need only "recall how incomparable and unique the life of every single saint is."[56] As the Holy Spirit moves the human mind, more and more creative means of manifesting the life of God open up for the human person.

Prudence, then, as mother of all the virtues, transforms knowledge of the truth of reality into practical expression in human affairs. This capacity to transform truth into action is most grievously impaired by a covetous spirit:

> Covetousness here means… immoderate straining for all the possessions which man thinks are needed to assure his own importance and status. Covetousness means an anxious senility, desperate self-preservation, overriding concern for confirmation and security. Need we say how utterly contrary such an attitude is to the fundamental bent of prudence; how impossible the informed and receptive silence of the subject before the truth of real things, how impossible just estimate and decision is, without a youthful spirit of brave trust and, as it were, a reckless tossing away of anxious self-preservation, a relinquishment of all egoistic bias toward mere confirmation of the self; how utterly, therefore, the virtue of prudence is

---

[56] Ibid., 38.

dependent upon the constant readiness to ignore the self, the limberness of real humility and objectivity?[57]

A man can only be prudent if all the powers of his soul are directed away from himself and towards the truth of real things. Unless he desires truth above and before his own (seeming) good, he cannot be prudent. We all know our capacity to distort the truth of real things to accord with our desires. Here, then, it becomes apparent how much prudence, the mother and form of all virtues, is in its turn dependent on the other virtues.[58] The virtues of justice, fortitude, and temperance need prudence to *inform* the passions with truth, but without justice, fortitude, and temperance, prudence would never be able to *move* the mind towards truth.

Justice

As with prudence, Pieper again and again emphasizes the "rank" of justice as the second of the cardinal virtues and the first of the strictly moral virtues (prudence is more an intellectual virtue than a moral virtue). Historically conditioned, he does so because of the emphasis on courage which was so frequently promoted by the Nazi regime to pressure people

---

[57] Ibid., 21.
[58] Cf. Ibid., 34

to support their cause. But courage, Pieper insisted, is for the sake of justice or it is not courage at all. Justice comes before courage and if its rank is not respected, dire consequences follow.

In our day, we, too, need a salutary reminder of the rank of justice. Because of the proliferation of sins against temperance, especially chastity, we are tempted to elevate these moderating and disciplining virtues to a higher rank. Yet doing so necessarily reduces these virtues to powers of mere restraint, rather than integrating capacities which preserve the desire for the joy of communion from dismantling the inner order of man. Only if justice, which orders man's relationships with others in accord with truth, maintains its rank as the highest of the moral virtues, can fortitude and temperance be true virtues as well.

This is all the more necessary when the rules of social interaction are being governed by tech companies bent on monetizing human relationships. We often consider "wasting time" on social media as an offense against temperance, which, of course, it is. But what would happen if we also recognized it as affront to justice, that not only does the inner order of man suffer as a consequence of binging on social media, but that the whole fabric of our relationships suffers? What vast horizons open up for us when we consider that pornography, for example, is not solely a sin against chastity, but against justice, and that it is a sin against chastity precisely because it is a sin against justice? Do we not, all of a sudden, recognize the personal dignity of the *other*, which excites in us a desire to order the desire to see another's beauty towards its true fulfillment in authentic communion?

If a virtuous life is man's great "yes" to his nature, the affirmation of who he is as man made in the image and likeness of God, then nowhere is this affirmation seen more visibly than in the realm of justice. For it belongs to justice to order man's relationships with others. Justice declares: man is not wholly himself as an isolated individual; he cannot manifest the life of the Trinitarian God coursing through his veins if he fails to live in harmonious communion with others. Only the just man lives in "conscious self-coordination with the direction of the movement of total reality," since only he is interiorly attuned to the communal nature of existence.

Justice orders man's relationships with others by giving to the other what is his due through an act of "restitution." This, perhaps more than anything else, reveals the personal structure in which man's active life unfolds, a structure that resists any once-and-for-all system of governance:

> The state of man's equilibrium that properly corresponds to man's essence, to his original, "paradisiac" state, is constantly thrown out of balance, and has constantly to be "restored" through an act of justice. Nor must the disturbance be necessarily understood

as injustice, though the fact that the act of justice is called *restitutio* presupposes that injustice is the prevalent condition in a world dominated by opposing interests, the struggle for power, and hunger.... [Yet] man's every act "disturbs" the stable equilibrium, since every act turns the doer into either a debtor or a creditor. And since men are constantly becoming indebted to one another, the demand is constantly raised to pay that debt by an act of "restitution." Therefore, the equality that characterizes justice cannot be finally and definitively established at any one time, it cannot be arrested. It must, rather, be constantly re-established, "restored anew."[59]

"Man's every act turns the doer into either a debtor or creditor." The other's very existence poses an obligation upon me. Justice cannot be accomplished in the world by merely setting up a just "system," (though, certainly, there is such a thing as just and unjust laws which either serve the common good or not), but by the communal recognition of our constant need to repay the other what is his due, and the resolve to do so.

Furthermore, because justice is in relation to the other, specifically as *other* (rather than as friend or relative), there

---

[59] Josef Pieper, "Justice" in *The Four Cardinal Virtues*, trans. Lawrence E. Lynch, 79-80.

is an emphasis on what is due to him as a *person*, rather than as this or that person. Thus, justice manifests the personal dimension of all life: "…we will find that not only justice but every moral obligation has a personal character, the character of the commitment to the person to whom I am under an obligation."[60] Man cannot escape the fact that he enters the world within a community and with obligations to the community and the other individuals within it. Every act of his in some way contributes to the flourishing of others and of society as a whole or detracts from it.

Finally, it should be clear that justice, as the virtue that orders man's relationships with others, is not sufficient of itself for the full flourishing of man and his community:

> We have already said that it is of the nature of communal life for men constantly to become indebted to each other and then just as constantly to pay one another the debt. We have further said that as a result the balance is in a constant state of shift and needs constantly to be restored to equilibrium…. It now remains for us to state that the world cannot be kept in order through justice alone…. The fact that some debts are not or cannot be paid is essential to the world's actual condition.[61]

---

[60] Ibid., 58.
[61] Ibid., 104.

At no point can a man tell his mother, "I owe you no more; we are even." Still less can man ever look at God and say, "I have paid you back; I have settled my account with you." Justice does not suffice in the matter of ordering man's relationships with others. And this is especially true in the most fundamental relationships of his life. Man can only live in relationship with others in a manner that accords with the truth of real things if he recognizes that "extravagance" is an essential element in living in accord with reality.

Precisely because the just man has a keen sense of what is due to another, he alone is able to live in the child-like freedom of effusively giving to another as much as he can: "There are obligations and debts which of their very nature cannot be adequately fulfilled and discharged. Only the just man takes pains to give each man his due, and only the just man, accordingly, fully experiences that disparity and undertakes to overcome it by some kind of 'excess.'"[62] The just man is not fixated on calculations, on "keeping the score," as it were ("I fast twice a week and pay tithes on all I get"). Rather, of all men, he is able to celebrate a feast, to offer sacrifice, to show mercy. For he feels deeply that the "movement of total reality" is a movement of unmerited and extravagant gift, and he strives with all the power of his nature to live in accord with that movement.

---

[62] Ibid., 110.

Fortitude

Perhaps the just man's awareness of the superfluity of all being is a fitting introduction to the virtue of fortitude. If all of man's life originates in the excessive love of God, man finds himself, before any other disposition, in a posture of receptivity. His life is not, strictly speaking, his. It is not "due" to him. It belongs to him as sheer gift. And nothing alerts man to this reality more than when he experiences the fullness of life in the encounter with love. Pieper's line of thought on this matter coincides precisely with that of his friend, Josef Ratzinger:[63] "How can we describe that moment in which we experience what life truly is? It is the moment of love, a moment which is simultaneously the moment of truth when life is discovered for what it is.... The discovery of life entails going beyond the I, leaving it behind. It happens only when one ventures along the path of self-abandonment, letting oneself fall into the hands of another."[64] Man discovers that his life is not truly his when he experiences his life in another; when he experiences the fullness of life offered in loving communion.

---

[63] Cf. Pieper, *Death and Immortality*, trans. Richard and Clara Winston (South Bend: St. Augustine's Press, 2000), 92.

[64] Ratzinger, *Eschatology: Death and Eternal Life*, trans. Michael Waldstein (Washington, D.C.: The Catholic University of America Press, 1988), 94.

Yet it is precisely in this awareness that man finds himself in a very vulnerable position: "...if the mystery of life is... identical with the mystery of love, it is, then, bound up with an event which we may call 'death-like.'"[65] In the experience of death, Ratzinger explains,

> Man is forced to face the fact that existence is not at his disposal, nor is his life his own property. Man may snap back defiantly that he will nevertheless try to acquire the power that will make it so. But in so doing, he makes a desperate anger his basic attitude to life. There is a second possibility: man can respond by seeking to trust this strange power to whom he is subject. He can allow himself to be led, unafraid, by the hand, without *Angst*-ridden concern for his situation. And in this second case, the human attitude towards pain, towards the presence of death within living, merges with the attitude we call love.
>
> As we know, people run up against the fact that life is not at their disposal in more forms than those of such physical limitations as sickness bring home to us. The same thing happens in the central region of the human landscape: our intimate ordination towards being loved. Love is the soul's true nourishment, yet this food which of all substances we most

---

[65] Ibid.

need is not something we can produce for ourselves. One must wait for it. The only way to make absolutely certain that one will *not* receive it is to insist on procuring it by oneself....

And so it turns out that the confrontation with physical death is actually a confrontation with the basic constitution of human existence. It places before us a choice: to accept either the pattern of love, or the pattern of power.[66]

If the just man, above all, recognizes that his life is sheer gift, he recognizes also that his life is supremely insecure in his own hands. His life is wholly in the hands of another. And in order to live in accord with the "movement of total reality," he must be able to suffer the experience of not being in control of his life. But this means being able to suffer the fear of death without "*Angst*-ridden concern for his situation." Failure to do so will result in the failure to experience the fullness of life in love. In the face of the horrifying possibility that he will not receive the gift of the beloved's presence, man must be able to stand firm in trust and resist the temptation to seize the beloved by his own power. Only then will he be able to receive his life as a gift.

This, then, is the role of fortitude in man's life. It is the disposition of the man who, in the face of the fear of death,

---

[66] Ibid., 96.

stands firm in the truth. Without fortitude, man cannot hope to be just because he is constantly threatened by the loss of what is his. And in his fear, he may take what is another's in an attempt to secure what is his own. Justice demands, however, that one be able to suffer the loss of one's own so that another may have what is his.

This is not to say that man is simply and absolutely to suffer the loss of what is his own. There is place for active resistance and attack which employs all the power of righteous anger in its service. What fortitude demands is that when such attack would disrupt the demands of justice, one must be able to cease his active resistance and, for the sake of justice, suffer evil: "the true 'position' of fortitude is that extremely perilous situation… in which to suffer and endure is objectively the only remaining possibility of resistance."[67] Yet in his suffering he reveals that love, rather than power, is the foundation of his life. What is really "real" in his life is not efficiency and practicality but love.

This virtue has particular relevance in a world which seems fixed on exposing the manifold forms of injustice around us. There is no question that such injustice is real and in need of healing. But in a technological world, the goal of which is to reduce to a minimum any and all forms of suffering in our lives, we think of healing injustice according to the

---

[67] Josef Pieper, "Fortitude" in *The Four Cardinal Virtues*, trans. Daniel F. Coogan, 128.

pattern of power. We think that fortitude should not be necessary, that the goal in our struggle against injustice should be to remove the need for fortitude in the world. The Christian, however, approaches the healing of injustice differently. He does not strive to make injustice absent, but to make love present. The removal of injustice is thus contextualized within the greater goal of increasing love. Only in this way can the removal of injustice be prevented from bringing about even greater injustices.

Fortitude thus shows itself most fully in martyrdom. The martyr rightly fears death: "One who has lost the will to live does not fear death.... [But] the brave man is not deluded: he sees that the injury he suffers is an evil. He does not undervalue and falsify reality; he 'likes the taste' of reality as it is, real; he does not love death nor does he despise life."[68] But he values his life less than he values truth. He does not give himself to suffering for its own sake, but only because he clings to the good, and such clinging entails suffering. Furthermore, he does not stumble upon suffering ignorantly or with a false sense of assurance. He holds fast to the good, knowing what this will cost him. He is purified of all false sense of heroism. The martyr is only revered after the fact: "In the final act of being courageous [the martyr] is put down, ridiculed,

---

[68] Ibid., 126.

abandoned, and, above all, silenced."[69] His final act looks like a failure. It looks like the real power in the world is that of injustice. Yet in this act of suffering, the martyr maintains his capacity to praise God, and so reveals that reality is and remains, beyond all appearances, good.

Nevertheless, while fortitude shows itself most fully in the martyr, there is a "mystic" fortitude that is requisite for every Christian. To "let go" of one's preconceived notions and natural certainties, confidently trusting that the Holy Spirit is leading one into Eternal Beatitude, is only possible if that same Holy Spirit emboldens one to "put on the mind of Christ," and live in the darkness of faith. Such mystic fortitude is especially necessary for a generation that wants to bring renewal to a Church which it sees weighed down by sins and malfunctioning institutions:

> Whenever a "new generation" takes up the attack against the resisting forces of evil or against a tense obsession with a security which clings to the delusion that the disharmony of the world is fundamentally curable by cautious and correct "tactics," it is above all necessary to maintain a lively and vigilant awareness that such fighting can only reach beyond sound and fury if it draws its strongest forces from the

---

[69] Josef Pieper, "Contemporary Relevance of the Cardinal Virtues" in *Exercises in the Elements: Essays – Speeches – Notes*, 111.

fortitude of the mystical life, which dares to submit unconditionally to the governance of God.[70]

Renewal is only possible if its source is the wisdom which comes from God. It is not by "great deeds" as perceived by the world, but by humble obedience to the Spirit of God that renewal can occur. St. John Vianney renewed the Church in France not by any regimented discipline able to be repeated by others, nor by boisterous accusation against the French clergy grievously compromised during the French Revolution, but by humble obedience to the Holy Spirit. Only such fortitude, which dares to let go of visible and tangible success, can bring renewal to the Church according to the pattern of love, rather than that of power.

Temperance

St. Thomas Aquinas assigns three objective characteristics to beauty: *integritas* (integrity or wholeness), *consonantia* (harmony), and *claritas* (brightness or radiance). Something is beautiful inasmuch as it is whole, its various parts harmonize with the whole, and its truth is perceivable to others. Everything that has been said in this chapter thus far has been said with an eye towards the beauty of the human being perfected in virtue. In restoring human nature to its original

---

[70] Pieper, "Fortitude" in *The Four Cardinal Virtues*, 140.

dignity by uniting it to God in the sacraments, God continues to make the Face of Christ, who is "the fairest of the children of men," present in the world. This restoration is made visible in prudence, justice, fortitude, and temperance, but above all, in temperance:

> It is not easy to read in a man's face whether he is just or unjust. Temperance or intemperance, however, loudly proclaim themselves in everything that manifests a personality: in the order or disorder of the features, in the attitude, the laugh, the handwriting. Temperance, as the inner order of man, can as little remain "purely interior" as the soul itself, and as all other life of the soul or mind. It is the nature of the soul to be the "form of the body."[71]

Temperance draws all of man's most basic drives for fulfillment into a harmonious whole, exteriorly manifesting the life of Christ within. Temperance thus makes one beautiful.

Sadly, this virtue, perhaps more than any other, has been emasculated in modern culture. Because of its capacity to render one beautiful, we are tempted to reduce the virility of temperance to a stagnated calculation of external moderation, to a polite conformity to social norms so that one may appear pleasing in the eyes of others. Such reduction leaves

---

[71] Pieper, "Temperance" in *The Four Cardinal Virtues*, 203.

no place for the power of wrath to manifest itself in loving protection of one's dignity, for the power of sexual desire to show itself in exuberant and sacrificial offerings of love, for the delight of human touch to manifest the joy of communion. Above all, this "emasculated concept of moderation has no place in a doctrine which asserts that the love of God – fountainhead of all virtues – knows neither mean nor moderation."[72] Temperance imparts beauty not because it conforms one to external standards of polite behavior, but because it unites all the disparate drives of the human psyche into a cohesive whole by directing them towards God. Temperance, consequently, is not, ultimately, about itself, but about "that crystal-clear, morning fresh freedom from self-consciousness…" which allows one to place God before oneself and so perceive reality as it is and live in accord with truth.

It is far beyond the scope of this book to examine all of the ways that temperance moderates and orders man's different desires (in the realm of eating, sexual desire, desire for glory and recognition, desire for greatness, etc.). But Pieper emphasizes one form in particular: the role of temperance in directing man's desire *to see*: "I am referring to the love of seeing, literally: seeing with our physical eyes."[73] Pieper's

---

[72] Ibid., 145-146.

[73] Pieper, "Contemporary Relevance of the Cardinal Virtues," 112.

emphasis on the literality of seeing is significant. Beauty, specifically physical beauty, awakens a passion that, "in the realm of the senses, which at first would seem to be the only adequate realm, can never be satisfied."[74] Through his capacity to see, man can experience a foretaste of fulfillment far surpassing any this-worldly joy. There is nothing man craves more than this vision.

Yet there is a condition: the capacity to be shaken outside of oneself, to be launched into a realm that exceeds human calculation and fabrication, depends wholly on man's capacity to approach beauty receptively. In other words, man cannot possibly see the invisible through the visible, the Infinite through the finite, if his desire to see is not ordered by the virtue of temperance. Pieper says repeatedly that the passion awakened by the vision of beauty must be "accepted and sustained in lasting purity."[75] It is a passion born in the sensitive realm, but it does not remain there. And as such, any attempt to confine the desire to see to what can be satisfied in the realm of the senses necessarily destroys the desire itself. Beauty can only fulfill its mission to shake man to his core and transport him to the heavenly sphere if it is perceived by a temperate spirit.

---

[74] Pieper, *"Divine Madness": Plato's Case Against Secular Humanism*, 49.

[75] Ibid., 37, 42, 50.

Pieper is under no illusions about the difficulty of such a task in our day: "The restoration of man's inner eyes can hardly be expected in this day and age unless, first of all, one were willing and determined simply to exclude from one's life all those inane and contrived but titillating illusions incessantly generated by the entertainment industry."[76] Thanks to the proliferation of sense stimuli, beauty is being removed from man's life. This is happening not because there are no beautiful objects presenting themselves to man, but because there are so many beautiful objects being presented to him that he thinks beauty can be manufactured and produced at will. He has forgotten that only temperance allows him to perceive beauty.

However, for the one who has this virtue, the desire that beauty awakens within him is "transformed into an attitude that leaves far behind all selfish desires and is most appropriately called a form of 'worship.'"[77] C.S. Lewis (whose influence is seen in many of Pieper's works) describes the power of beauty to effect this transformation, which is at once terrifying and beatifying, in a magnificent scene in *Till We have Faces*. The main character makes her "complaint against the gods" for taking from her the one love she had in her life. She remonstrates: "Do you think we mortals will find you gods

---

[76] Pieper, "Learning How to See Again" in *Only the Lover Sings*, 33.

[77] Pieper, *Divine Madness*, 55.

easier to bear if you're beautiful? I tell you that if that's true we'll find you a thousand times worse. For then (I know what beauty does) you'll lure and entice. You'll leave us nothing; nothing that's worth our keeping or your taking. Those we love best – whoever's most worth loving – those are the very ones you'll pick out."[78] In the encounter with beauty, she acknowledges, sacrificial self-offering is the only appropriate response. Worship flows forth from the soul of one who is capable of being moved by beauty.

Finally, Pieper again emphasizes the "ranking" of temperance among the four cardinal virtues. In an age when material comforts abound, it is important for the one who wants to resist worldly temptations to remember that discipline is not good in and of itself. Certainly, there is a very pressing need to deny oneself the little luxuries that are continually offered to us, lest our desire for pleasure control us. And everyone knows how easy it is to make excuses so as to gratify our self-indulgent desires. Nevertheless, temperance remains the fourth of the cardinal virtues. Discipline is not for its own sake, but for the sake of living in accord with the truth. St. Thomas argues that "the person who, beside the dictate of right reason, abstains from all pleasure through aversion, as

---

[78] C.S. Lewis, *Till We Have Faces* (Orlando: Harcourt, 1984), 290.

it were, for pleasure as such, is insensible as a country lout."[79] If prudence demands that, for the sake of justice, one must eat a sumptuous dinner provided by his host, it is a failure of temperance if he denies himself that pleasure. Likewise, if one chooses to remain a virgin for his whole life, not out of love for Christ, but because he has an aversion towards sexual pleasure (which, incidentally, is the context for St. Thomas' quote), his virginity cannot be called virtuous despite the discipline it requires. Once again, the beauty of temperance consists in its rightly ordering man's desires according to the truth.

And so it is that we see in the encounter with beauty the interconnectivity of all the virtues. Temperance allows man to experience the power of the *passio amoris* – the passion of love – enkindled by beauty, without that power destroying him by its being reduced to selfish grasping; fortitude makes him capable of suffering the loss of all for the sake of the beauty he has beheld; both of these virtues preserve his capacity to rightly give what is "due" in justice to the beauty he beholds; and in doing so, man lives the truth by prudently directing all his powers towards the goal given him in faith, which is union with God. Through the virtues, man's whole being radiates the presence of Christ. And, like Christ, the

---

[79] Thomas Aquinas, *Summa Theologiae*, Latin text edited and translated by Laurence Shapcote (Lander, Wyoming: Aquinas Institute for the Study of Sacred Doctrine, 2012), II-II, 152, 2 ad 2.

virtuous man is passionate because he lives in love. He lives energetically in accord with the movement of total reality as he consciously coordinates his actions together with the movement of all things towards God, their true goal. This movement, as we shall see in the next two chapters, is none other than that which is expressed and actualized in celebration of the Sacred Liturgy.

Chapter 3

Embodying Christ

"Veiled Beauty"

Veiled.
Yet for all that,
Not concealed.
The mystery hidden within
Unveils itself, still veiled,
To one who sees.

Your covering
Like the night bespeaks
Intimacy,
Enchanting those who long to see
Infinite Love
In finitude.

This world,
Parched for such love,
Unveils all and so lays bare
Its emptiness.
Exiled souls thus stand
Exposed.
O radiant Bride and Mother!
O Bearer of the Godhead
In your flesh!
The eternal feminine revealing
Eternity;
Joy to one who sees.

In *The Voyage of the Dawn Treader*, C.S. Lewis imagines an island in the land of Narnia on which a magician lives. Lucy, a 10-year-old girl, is tasked with sneaking into the magician's house, finding his book of spells, and reading a spell that makes hidden things visible. As she flips through the book of spells, she comes across one that would make her "beautiful beyond the lot of mortals." [80] The book even depicts for her what she would look like if she were to say the spell; and indeed, she finds herself fearsomely beautiful. Lucy is sorely tempted, especially because of her jealousy towards her older sister who has always been considered "the pretty one" in the family. She is saved from her temptation, but it pains her to have seemingly lost the chance of being made so beautiful.

Lucy eventually finds the spell to make hidden things visible. As she reads it, Aslan – the joy of her heart and the figure of Christ in Lewis' books – becomes apparent to her. Lewis tells us that, beholding Aslan, Lucy's "face lit up till, for a moment (but of course she didn't know it), she looked almost as beautiful as that other Lucy in the picture…"[81] Lucy received the beauty she longed for, not by a spell, but by the encounter

---

[80] C.S. Lewis, *The Voyage of the Dawn Treader* in *The Chronicles of Narnia* (New York: Harper Collins, 2001), 495.
[81] Ibid., 498.

with a divine lover. The awareness of his presence made her "beautiful beyond the lot of mortals."

There is in us something like a nostalgia for our true self. In Christ, we see the beauty of human nature joined to the divine. We glimpse what we could be as all that is human – mind, will, and body – works together harmoniously in its movement towards God. Captivated by the beauty of Christ, we wonder what we need to do to attain this same beauty. Will some spell, some perfectly planned regimen of life, do the trick?

There is actually a danger in beholding the beauty of Christ and attempting to attain it by our own power. Pieper argues that the one *more* self-possessed, more "virtuous" in a sense, is in more danger of committing mortal sin than the one who is weak:

> [T]he more spiritual a human being is, that is, the more he has rendered himself immune to the seductions and charms of the sensible world by living a life of self-abnegation and disciplining his will, the more he can now commit *the* offense, the sin of unadulterated hybris and blatant pride. Only if all the powers of my being obey me does the question suddenly occur to me: whom do I myself now obey?[82]

---

[82] Pieper, *The Concept of Sin*, 62.

The contemporary scholar Erasmo Leiva-Merikakis gives a haunting depiction of this, commenting on Christ's teaching about the demon, driven from a soul, who returns and brings more demons with it: "It seems that the heart has renounced evil, but only in its grosser manifestations. Its beauty is really only superficial, cosmetic… because the dynamism of evil has been followed by an empty neutrality: after the tyrannical 'strong man' has been driven out, no new master was welcomed to sit here at table, no new energy received to communicate life, joy, and hope."[83] The beauty of the virtuous life does not consist solely in driving out the tyrannical power of inordinate passions, but in giving oneself over to another power, that of God's supreme governance.

Flourishing through Love

Like it was for Lucy, so it is for us. The beauty we see in Christ is not some external model for us to attain, but rather something that happens to us interiorly when our human nature suffers the presence of the divine. We see this dynamic at play in participatory fashion within the context of human relationships. In being loved by another, one has the experience of flourishing, of becoming more fully oneself. The lover

---

[83] Erasmo Leiva-Merikakis, *Fire of Mercy, Heart of the Word: Meditations on the Gospel according to St. Matthew, Vol. II* (San Francisco: Ignatius Press, 2003), 162.

seems to call the beloved's true self forth from him. This is because only the lover "may succeed in perceiving the beloved's very purpose in being."[84] The joy of love consists in being known intimately. Despite all his faults and shortcomings, the beloved sees, reflected to him in the perceptive eyes of the lover, who he truly is. And he suddenly becomes capable of living according to that truth. For a moment, for as long as he suffers the lover's gaze, he finds himself truly capable of virtue.[85] He remembers, as it were, what it means to be human; and he longs for that true self to last.

Tim McGraw's song "I like it, I love it," playfully articulates the power of this love, while also revealing another dimension. He sings, "my mama and my daddy tried to teach me courtesy, but it never sank in till that girl got a hold of me. Now I'm holdin' umbrellas and opening up doors, I'm taking out the trash and I'm sweeping my floor..." The singer "knew" that it was good for him to be courteous and responsible. What he lacked was not knowledge of the good. What he lacked was a presence somehow capable of drawing the good out of him.

We see here that the lover does not draw the good out of the beloved simply by seeing his "purpose in being" and wanting him to live according to that purpose. To be sure, the

---

[84] Pieper, "On Love," 182.
[85] Ibid., 183.

lover, precisely because she knows the truth of the beloved, cannot affirm him for being less than his true self. She loves him too much for that. She knows the goodness of the beloved and longs to see that good *in concreto* in his actions. In this sense, the lover can be quite demanding of the beloved. Simply by seeing the truth of who he is, the lover calls the beloved to conversion by her penetrating gaze.

Nevertheless, the lover succeeds in beautifying the beloved not primarily by her simple good will towards him. It is not enough for her to merely say, "I know you; you are good." Rather, the beloved must experience the *unio affectus* of the lover, the desire of the lover to be united to the good that she beholds, even "in fact to identify with him."[86] This is the distinctly *personal* quality of love. The beloved does not experience himself as a project that the lover takes upon herself to make him better. Rather, he experiences himself as a *person* to whose fullness the lover desires to be united, having intuited that fullness in her loving gaze.

Christ, then, transforms our own human nature not by externally fixing it, but by opening it from within to the divine presence. In the *presence of Christ*, man becomes fully himself. "Being Christian," Pope Benedict XVI wrote, "is not the result of an ethical choice or a lofty idea, but the encounter with an event, a person, which gives life a new horizon

---

[86] Ibid., 196-197.

and a decisive direction."[87] In the presence of Christ, the Incarnate Logos, man has the experience of the divine lover who desires to be united to his creatures. Man finds himself known and affirmed in the depths of his being. And being so known and affirmed, he submits himself entirely to the One who loves him so much, and so becomes capable of living according to the truth of who he is.

The Visibility of Divine Love

How Christ submits human nature to the governance of God is significant. "First of all, what is lovable must have revealed itself to our eyes, to our sensuous as well as mental faculty of perception: 'Visio est quaedam causa amoris', seeing is a kind of cause of love."[88] Because Christ has revealed the love of God to us *in our flesh*, the flesh itself becomes capable of drawing us to God. Pieper references the Preface of Mass for the Nativity of the Lord: "In the mystery of the Word made Flesh, a new light of your glory has shone upon the eyes of our mind, so that, as we recognize in him God made visible, we may be caught up through him in love of things in-

---

[87] Pope Benedict XVI, *Deus Caritas Est* (Washington, D.C.: United States Conference of Catholic Bishops, 2005), 1.
[88] Pieper, "On Love," 197.

visible."[89] In this prayer, Pieper argues, the Church states that the capacity for rapture, to be taken away from the present moment and brought into the presence of God, depends upon an experience available to our senses.

This may seem strange to those who want to make a clear and distinct separation between the finite and the Infinite, the visible and the invisible. What is presented to the senses is finite. And so, it would seem, if man wishes to behold the Infinite, he should train himself to be detached from finite realities and learn to contemplate the invisible "forms" alone. The visible world – above all, the body – seems to be a hindrance to beholding the invisible world. The senses must be denied so that we may perceive what cannot be sensed.

There is, of course, truth in this statement. If we cling solely to what can be sensed, we will never behold what lies outside sense experience. Healthy detachment from the senses, fostered by arduous asceticism, is necessary for one to transcend the limitations of the finite world.

Nevertheless, according to Pieper, it is precisely the power of eros, the power of desirous love awakened by physical beauty, that opens man's eyes to perceive something beyond the physical realm. Indeed, without eros, he argues,

---

[89] *The Roman Missal*, English Translation According to the Third Typical Edition (Washington, DC: United States Conference of Catholic Bishops, 2011), 390.

such love for the Infinite would be incomplete: "Thomas Aquinas is equally convinced that neither 'elevated' nor 'spiritual' love… can become a living reality without the *passio amoris*, that is, without the soul's being moved by concrete sensory presence."[90] The one so moved by physical beauty has a longing for… he knows not what. His vision of what *can be* comprehended has awakened in his heart a longing for something that *cannot be* comprehended. "Seeing is a kind of cause of love." And the love that can be aroused by physical sight has the power to expand man's vision to behold something more than what can be seen. The one who suffers the *passio amoris* longs for something, but what he longs for is *not* that which he sees with his eyes.

It is precisely in this way that the longing for what is invisible can come to us through what is visible. The concrete, visible reality presented to us becomes a sign that points to a fulfillment found in an invisible reality:

> The essence of beauty… precisely does not consist in providing satisfaction, like something that "gratifies," no matter how highly spiritual a gratification it may be. Goethe, rather surprisingly, captured this… notion in an admirably succinct sentence: "Beauty is not so much a fulfillment as rather a promise." In other

---

[90] Pieper, *Divine Madness*, 53.

words, by absorbing beauty with the right disposition, we experience, not gratification, satisfaction, and enjoyment but the arousal of an expectation; we are oriented toward something "not-yet-here." He who submits properly to the encounter with beauty will be given the sight and taste not of a fulfillment but of a promise – a promise that, in our bodily existence, can never be fulfilled.[91]

The experience of the presence of God, of rapturous longing for the Infinite, comes to embodied spiritual creatures not apart from physical realities, but precisely through them.

Certainly, this "rapture" does not happen automatically or even by human choice. Beauty chooses to reveal herself to man; man's choice consists in his receptivity to divine election. Pieper argues that one must absorb physical beauty *with the right disposition*. One must open himself up to remembrance, he says, must allow beauty to remind him of his true self.[92] And this remembrance, perhaps, is more difficult to suffer than might be expected. If "rapture" reminds someone that his true destiny is found in a reality that transcends the finite world, he will likely find it extremely uncomfortable to experience such remembrance. In our finite world, keeping

---

[91] Pieper, *Divine Madness*, 47-48.
[92] Cf. Pieper, *Divine Madness*, 47.

oneself empty enough to be satisfied solely by the Infinite is a truly heroic affair. But there is another, more hidden, reason that the remembrance awakened by beauty is difficult to suffer.

Because one's true self is unknown except to the lover, one must surrender control over his own self-understanding and instead *receive* his identity from another. And this is a most discomfiting experience. Pieper explains:

> At bottom all love is undeserved. We can neither earn it nor promote it; it is always pure gift. It is even… the "prime gift" that makes all other gifts possible. *But there seems to be in man something like an aversion for receiving gifts.* No one is wholly unfamiliar with the thought: I don't want anything for nothing! And this emotion comes uncannily close to the other: I don't want to be "loved," and certainly not for no reason![93]

In the experience of love, one knows that nothing he has done has *earned* the affection of the other. His personal qualities may be the condition of the other's affection for him, but they have not caused it. And this experience is unsettling. In the experience of love, one feels that he is not in control of

---

[93] Pieper, "On Love," 179 [emphasis added].

the other's affirmation of his being. This most life-giving experience is wholly dependent on the other's free gift of self.

Because this is the case, one who refuses to receive his life as a gift will be saddened by having been made for the joy of love. He will not want to suffer the gaze of the lover who alone manages to perceive the beloved's purpose in being. He will not open himself up to remembrance of his true self. Rather, he will want to project his own self-understanding upon others' perception of him, subtly controlling what others are drawn to in him. In fear, he will not allow himself to be laid bare, lest he experience the rejection of his deepest self (which is a veritable foretaste of Hell). In the experience of love awakened by beauty, then, he will recoil from the deepest truth about himself. He will seek affirmation not in truth, not as he is as a creature, but as he projects himself to be.

The disposition necessary, then, for one to be "caught up in love of things invisible" through "God made visible," is that of childlike wonder before the mystery of creation. The child, free from all preconceived notions and ideas, free from any self-made personas, has the ability to receive his identity from another. According to Erasmo Leiva-Merikakis, "the child symbolizes the human capacity to allow oneself to be taken care of by another, even to be *carried* by another into a new, mysterious realm never before explored..."[94] The Incarnation invites man to approach creation not in the analytical posture of the examiner, looking for something specific, but in the receptive posture of a child who knows not what he seeks. The lover and the child are united in their capacity to be taken away from the here-and-now and brought by another to an encounter with what is beyond their comprehension. And only in that encounter does man become fully himself, "beautiful beyond the lot of mortals."

Christ, then, submits humanity to the governance of God by embracing the limitations of human existence in the world. The finite is the gate leading to the Infinite. If, in chapter two, we saw that man is made beautiful by being directed towards God, here we see that such direction is only possible for one who perceives God in the finite. Only he can be touched by God in every facet of his humanity.

And although he draws from Plato in his remarks about eros and physical beauty, Pieper argues that this affirming approach to the visible world of the senses finds its ultimate justification in the Incarnation: "it is impossible to understand the fundamental reality of the Christian faith, the Incarnation of the Logos, without accepting the truth that the visible

---

[94] Erasmo Leiva-Merikakis, *Fire of Mercy, Heart of the Word: Meditations on the Gospel According to Saint Matthew, Volume Three* (San Francisco: Ignatius Press, 2012), 111 [emphasis original].

world and even the 'flesh' in which Adam became weak, is fundamentally good."[95] Only because all that can be presented to our sense experience is fundamentally good can it be a fit dwelling place for divinity. Only the one who affirms the goodness of his creaturely existence, with all its limitations and dependencies, can experience rapture, can experience the presence of God in the world. In the Incarnation, God became man, hidden within the womb of Mary. From now on, if we run from our limitedness, we find ourselves running from God.

Acedia and the Flight from Divine Beauty

This embracing of our limitedness is all the more challenging in an age that seeks "to make the whole of reality a field of raw material for the exploitation of utilitarian plans."[96] The material world, it seems, is good only to the extent that it serves man's will to power. The technological tendency of modern man is to stretch the limits of the material world – to beat it into submission, as it were – so that it may more efficiently actualize the desires of the autonomous human will. We do not see the material world as *given*, as

---

[95] Josef Pieper, "Creation and Sacrament" in *Traditional Truth, Poetry, Sacrament*, trans. Daniel Farrelly (South Bend: St. Augustine's Press, 2019), 216.

[96] Pieper, "What Does "Academic" mean?" 36.

establishing the very conditions for flourishing humanity. Rather, we see it as something whose limitations are to be overcome *so that* we may flourish. The human person finds fulfillment to the extent that his mind, his spirit, has its way; the body is a separate thing to be discarded, played with, or altered, depending on what one wants.

Pieper, instead, holds that "man is a 'built structure,' or, more precisely, that man is both spiritual and physical *at the same time* – so much so that there can be nothing in man that is 'purely spiritual' and nothing that is 'purely material.'"[97] "*Anima forma corporis*," he says, expressing the traditional phrase which articulates the soul's relationship to the body, "the soul is the *form* that gives shape to the body and the body is that which is formed by the soul."[98] The limitations that the body places on man do not hinder his fulfillment, but are the very conditions given to him to find fulfillment. Only in and through the body can man know another. If the body is treated as external to man, he will never encounter the *person* of the other – that by which he is created in the image and likeness of God – in a real way. Rather, he will perceive the body through his senses, and the person through his mind.

---

[97] Pieper, "Sign and Symbol as the Language of Christian Faith," 67.
[98] Ibid.

The personhood of the other, then, will not be experienced, but only "thought about."

We see this daily in our experience of driving. Rarely do people simply "go for a drive" anymore. Rather, while driving, our whole goal is to arrive at our destination as quickly as possible. Our cars and highways are designed to move us as efficiently as possible, and we become angered (even, sometimes, irate) when that efficiency of movement is disrupted. We know, as an idea, that other persons worthy of respect are in the cars around us. But our senses do not seem to get the message. What they experience are not persons, but obstacles, hindrances to our freedom of movement. The limitations that come with moving around in the physical world are problems to be solved, it seems, not helpful reminders that we are creatures, not God. In the case of driving, the limitations to our movement imposed by others' physical presence are signs reminding us that in the car next to us is the presence of a person, whose dignity cannot be reduced to utilitarian efficiency. But the more we live with the goal of removing the obstacles imposed by our embodied existence, the more others' personhood is obscured.

And just as others' personhood is experienced only in and through the body, so also is our experience of God contingent upon our embodied perception. For Pieper, the material world is so much a part of man's nature that one's relationship to it will determine his relationship to God. If man experiences the material world, the world accessible to his bodily senses, solely as an arena for commercial interests, for what lies wholly within his power to buy, sell, and manipulate, he will never be taken away in rapture by what can be presented to his senses. Which is to say that man will not be able to encounter God if the material world cannot somehow be experienced as a sign pointing to something – someone – beyond itself.[99]

Because our habituated approach to the world is technological/analytical, rather than contemplative and childlike, there is a particular difficulty for modern man to approach reality in this way. We do not know how to encounter symbols.[100] A sanctuary lamp, indicating the presence of the Eucharist in the tabernacle, may as well be an electric light rather than a burning candle, we think. It is more cost effective and basically does the same thing. And yet a candle, precisely because of its more limited nature, is more of a symbol than a light bulb. Precisely its *lack* of efficiency brings one into a world of non-utilitarian goods. Some things are worth giving one's all, just as a candle can only give light by its self-offering. The candle thus says, "there is something here, the proper

---

[99] Cf. Josef Pieper, "Down-to-Earth Contemplation" in *Problems of Modern Faith: Essays and Addresses*, trans. Jan van Huerck (Chicago: Franciscan Herald Press, 1985), 152.

[100] Cf. Pieper, "Sign and Symbol as the Language of Christian Faith," 63.

response to which is sacrificial self-offering." And it does so not by "saying" this to our mind, but by presenting itself to our senses.

For one who lives solely (or at least, habitually) within the utilitarian world, the language of sign and symbol will always remain foreign to him. He may understand the ideas communicated through the sign, but he will not experience the reality they communicate. For such a one, God may remain an idea in his mind, but He will not be the substance of his life. For that to happen, one must grow in fluency in speaking the language of sign and symbol, which is the language of the Incarnation, the language of Christian faith.

For Pieper, underlying man's imprisonment within the utilitarian world is the spiritual malady known as *acedia*: "Metaphysically and theologically," he explains, "the notion of *acedia* means that a man does not, in the last resort, give the consent of his will to his own being; that beneath the dynamic activity of his existence, he is still not at one with himself; that, as the Middle Ages expressed it, sadness overwhelms him when he is confronted with the divine goodness immanent in himself..."[101] Man's true greatness consists in his capacity to receive God, and so to receive one's very self in the penetrating gaze of Infinite Love. And he experiences this greatness precisely in his limitedness, in recognizing his

---

[101] Ibid., 44.

dependent nature as a creature. Because of the difficulty of living in such dependence, man can rebel against his own nature and live in the sadness of self-rejection.

Acedia, then, is sadness at having been made for the glory of God; at having been made to be seen by God, to be laid bare before Him as only a lover can lay one bare. To protect himself from the Lover's gaze, the person afflicted by *acedia* will not approach created reality as a sign, but only as an object of analysis. He will always need to understand, to "see through" things with perfect clarity rather than suffer mysteries, since what is mysterious is necessarily out of his control. He will "lay bare" the mystery, not in a reverent posture of contemplation, but in the tense posture of the examiner.[102]

This "laying bare" is, in fact, a defense mechanism to protect oneself from remembrance of one's true self. The one saddened by his creaturely existence becomes angered by whatever reminds him of it. If there is something or someone that is specifically set apart from the utilitarian world to direct one's gaze towards the divine, the person afflicted by *acedia* will want to desecrate it, will want to bring it back into the commercial world. Doing so keeps him safe from the claims the Infinite makes upon him. Pieper quotes Plato: "Few there are who remember… the sacred things they once

---

[102] Josef Pieper, "What Does it mean to Philosophize" in *For the Love of Wisdom*, 40.

beheld."[103] In flight from beauty, man surrounds himself with trivialities and, removing reminders of the Infinite from his perception, drowns himself in a stupor of forgetfulness.

The Sacredness of Creation

Because of beauty's capacity to remind man of his true self in relation to the Infinite, it is closely associated with the sacred. "The terms *holy* and *sacred*," Pieper says, "are used to mean certain tangible things, spaces, times, and actions as possessing the specific quality of being separated from the ordinary and directed toward the realm of the divine."[104] In their being set apart from the commercial world for the sake of the divine, these perceptible realities communicate an "intensified" divine presence.[105] While any encounter with beauty – a sunset, a mountain stream, a beloved face – has the power to enrapture someone, what is sacred is set apart explicitly to do so.

We see this concretely in the life of actor, Sir Alec Guinness. While he was in France filming *Father Brown*, the actor, dressed as a priest, caught the attention of a young boy. The

---

[103] Plato, quoted in Pieper, *Divine Madness*, 44.

[104] Pieper, "The Sacred and its Negation" in *In Search of the Sacred*, trans. Lothar Krauth (San Francisco: Ignatius Press, 1991), 22-23.

[105] Cf. ibid., 24.

boy approached the actor, took his hand, and began talking to him friendly as they walked. After a while, the boy simply waved goodbye and left. The confidence and affection of the boy left a deep impression on Guinness, eventually leading to his conversion to Catholicism. It was not for any moral holiness that the boy was drawn to the actor, nor because of any external beauty, but because, seeing Guinness dressed as a priest, he beheld the visible presence of God in the world. Anyone who has been in public with a religious sister knows this power of the sacred to draw someone to the divine. As a visible symbol of God's presence in the world, one who is set apart for God has the power to enrapture someone, to take someone away from the here-and-now and transport him into the realm of the divine.

Again, however, we must note that this rapture does not happen automatically or even very often. Rarely does someone walk into Mass and fall to the ground in wonder at the Mystery of the Incarnate God's Presence hidden in the form of bread and wine. One must approach the sacred symbols with the right disposition, namely, faith. By faith, one maintains a childlike posture before God which allows him to be led by divine revelation not because it "makes sense," or because it conforms to one's ideas, but simply because God has said it.[106] Thus, faith places man in a position which is the

---

[106] Cf. Josef Pieper, "On Faith," 31.

exact opposite of that cultivated by our technological mindset. Without negating the place of the scientific/technological in human life, faith sets boundaries to its prominence. It does not forbid that man should have mastery and control over the material world; it only demands that such mastery serve the true good of man, which is his capacity to encounter God in the world.

The presence of sacred symbols, therefore, even as it limits the sphere of the utilitarian in one's life, expands the material world to hold the Infinite. Paradigmatically, Mary's consecrated virginity did not diminish her physical beauty, but rather made her body "Platytera," as the Byzantine Icon (depicted on this book's cover) proclaims. Using an expression we would not normally use to flatter a woman, we say that her body is "More Spacious" than the Heavens, capable of attracting men to the Infinite God precisely because she withdrew herself from the utilitarian world for the sake of God. Just so the Church, by using the language of sign and symbol to express Herself, reveals the deepest truth of her being: that She is the dwelling place of God in the world.

Silence: The Final Revelation

By inviting those who wish to hear her revelation to adopt the posture of faith so that they may understand her language, the Church brings with her an air of silence. This silence, however, does not bespeak emptiness, but rather superabundance. Pieper contrasts the analytical approach to reality with the example of St. Thomas Aquinas' final words. No one could fault St. Thomas for failing to approach the mysteries of the faith with a desire to better understand them. Nevertheless, St. Thomas ends his life in silence, refusing to continue his great theological work:

> The last word of St. Thomas is not communication but silence. And it is not death which takes the pen out of his hand. His tongue is stilled by the superabundance of life in the mystery of God. He is silent, not because he has nothing further to say; he is silent because he has been allowed a glimpse into the inexpressible depths of that mystery which is not reached by any human thought or speech.[107]

---

[107] Josef Pieper, "On Thomas Aquinas," in *The Silence of St. Thomas*, 38. Admittedly, there are other explanations of his silence which involve both physical and mental exhaustion or a head injury. Pieper, for his part, accepted the more hagiographical account of his silence coming as a result of a mystical encounter with

Often it is silence, rather than speech, that communicates depth of meaning. If we are to approach creation symbolically, we need to learn the role of silence in life.

Pieper demonstrates this awareness in his own life when discussing the final days of his beloved wife's life. In 1984, shortly before her death, Pieper's wife whispered words to her husband which deeply affected him. Certainly, there were many expressions of her love which she told him throughout their long marriage of 49 years. But these words had a profound impact. What those words were, we will never know.

Pieper describes the occasion with fitting solemnity:

> One afternoon she wanted me to sit beside her because she wanted to say something important; she was speaking with unusual seriousness. And then she put her arm around my shoulder and said something which I will never forget. But first you must know a story which only later became clear to me. Presumably she could not forget a conversation she had had almost a decade ago with the wife of my brother who had died unexpectedly. She regretted, and also found

---

God. Torrell offers a more critical account of his final days of relative silence. Cf. Jean-Pierre Torrell, O.P., *Saint Thomas Aquinas: Volume 1: The Person and His Work*, revised edition, trans. Robert Royal (Washington, D.C.: The Catholic University of America, 2005), 289-295.

surprising, that her husband had died without any goodbyes. At the time, I had listened to the women and said that when one is confronted so suddenly with the possibility of one's impending death one is understandably totally preoccupied and there is no place for any other thought. Clearly she did not want it to reach this point; she would not want to miss this moment for anything. She felt that she herself was going downhill and she feared that one day perhaps she would not be able to think and speak clearly any longer. So she probably was thinking of that conversation when she put her arm around my shoulder and said a single wonderful sentence *for no one's ear but mine*.[108]

In his love for his wife, Pieper refused to expose her words of love, spoken with the solemn awareness of approaching death, to the winds of the masses, lest such winds extinguish the flame that gently burned within him. The intimate exchange between Pieper and his wife belonged within a certain context which formed the very content of that exchange. Outside of that relational context, her words fail to

---

[108] Josef Pieper, *A Journey to Point Omega: Autobiography from 1964*, trans. Dan Farrelly (South Bend: St. Augustine's Press, 2020), 185-186 (emphasis mine).

communicate what she had communicated to her husband. And so the content of this beautiful exchange died with Pieper. And it is right that it should have done so. Indeed, it did so of necessity.

For Pieper, if we are going to foster a spirit that disposes us to approach creation sacramentally, we need to learn again the role of silence in our lives and in our relationships. Only in silence do we learn the posture that enables us to suffer the gaze of the lover. We finally drop the exhausting effort of "putting ourselves forward," as it were, making sure we are presentable, and can finally be laid bare before the other's eyes. Perhaps this is why Pieper says that the martyr is the one who is, "above all, silenced." In his heroic act of courage, the martyr finally succeeds in "putting on Christ" in his death, entrusting himself without reserve to the love of the Father.

The Church, speaking the language of sign and symbol, wraps in silence those who come to her in faith. And in that silence, one hears again the voice of the Creator speaking over His creation: "it is good." Indeed, one experiences his own life as very good because he encounters, in visible form, the living God whose love holds him in existence. Pieper was keenly aware of the healing effect the Church has for a people that has sold itself to the utilitarian world:

the more the absolutist claim of what is merely utilitarian threatens to confiscate our entire existence, the more the human being, if he is going to live a genuinely humane life, needs this opportunity to step away occasionally from this tumult of sights and sounds ("buy this, drink that, eat those, amuse yourself here, demonstrate for or against") away from this unremitting experience of being screamed at, and to emerge in a place where silence prevails and thus, real hearing becomes possible, listening to that reality upon which our existence rests and from which it is continually nourished and renewed.[109]

Only in silence can the human heart hear the voice of the Creator, through which man finds his true meaning and direction in life.

Conclusion

In the movie *Arrival*, extraterrestrials come to earth and begin attempting to communicate with humans. A linguist,

---

[109] Josef Pieper, quoted by Bernard Schumacher in "A Cosmopolitan Hermit: An Introduction to the Philosophy of Josef Pieper" in *A Cosmopolitan Hermit: Modernity and Tradition in the Philosophy of Josef Pieper*, ed. Bernard Schumacher (Washington, D.C.: The Catholic University of America Press, 2009), 19.

Louise Banks, is recruited to learn the language and so decipher what the aliens are saying. As she studies the language, she begins having memories of her future daughter. These memories increase as she becomes more fluent in the language. What she discovers is that the language of the aliens articulates a non-linear perception of the world. They see things differently than humans, and so they express that reality differently. And the more Louise learns that language, the more she sees things as they do.

Christianity perceives reality from the perspective of the Incarnation, of God's intimate indwelling in creation. God has chosen to communicate the mystery of his own Life in the weakness of human flesh. The Incarnation is, as it were, the "language" God uses to speak to man. The Church, having learned that language, sees reality as God does; Life is found not in power, but in self-giving love. And so the Church uses finite signs and symbols to communicate the Infinite to man. By setting apart what is human and earthly for the sake of divine worship, the Church enraptures man so that, beholding God's Presence in the world, he might become fully himself.

Modernity has made it difficult for us to learn this language of sign and symbol. Saddened that the finite has been created to house the Infinite, modernity's language is one of technological dominance. Speaking this language, we no longer hear the voice of the Creator, but only of the autonomous human will. Creation speaks of itself alone. The echo of a Voice, beckoning us to transcend the limits of this world, is drowned out by the clamorous sounds of utilitarian function. Beauty is hidden; and so man has forgotten himself.

The Church, like Christ, is vulnerable in such a world. Her voice will inevitably be lost in a world of utilitarian function unless She is protected by divine power. And this power, according to Pieper, flows from the font of the Sacred Liturgy. Only if She is given to divine worship can the Church hope to successfully communicate the truth of her being to the world: the truth that real power is found not in strength but in weakness, in the surrender of self to another in love.

Chapter 4

Celebrating Christ

"Repose in Exile"

A truly painful Stillness,
Which in Communion lies,
Descending from the Heights above
Gives birth to all our sighs.

The braying barks of business
Are far less jarring than
The Gentle Breeze that Beckons
And calls us Home again.

Surely we must concoct
Cacophonous concerns,
Lest God who draws us upwards
Our commerce overturns.

The enchanting Voice of Gladness,
The alluring sight of Play,
Forgetful of the world outside,
Our exiled hearts betray.

Can such a world exist,
That knows no fear of Hell,
Where endless Joy awaits,
And songs of Triumph swell?
Safer to dwell in bondage,
Subject to finite ends,

Than spend our meager earnings
On a Hope that here transcends.

And yet to see our Homeland
And hear its joyful strains,
While we in exile languish,
Would e'en now unbind our chains.

The Stillness, then, continues
To haunt each weary heart
Till Heav'n and Earth are joined again,
A Communion ne'er to part.

In ancient Thrace, Thales of Milet was caught up in wonder at the beauty of the stars above as he walked along a road. Engaged in contemplation, he failed to see a well directly in his path, and he plummeted down the pit. A Thracian maidservant, witnessing his fall, laughed at him in mockery. "That is for Plato," according to Pieper, "the typical reaction of robust everyday common sense to philosophy."[110] The maidservant, representative of "the masses" who judge the world by the standards of efficiency and productivity, will always find the lover of wisdom absurd. What good is all his contemplation if it leads him into pits? Better to attend to the "real" world here within one's grasp.

An occupational hazard of the contemplative is that he will sometimes lose his bearing in the world of practical affairs. A man may intend to pass through a city when, struck by the beauty of a man's search for God, he changes his plans entirely and stays at the man's house that day for supper. Or he may be so caught up by the tragedy of man's brokenness in the world, manifest in the withered hand of a man at a synagogue, that he reaches out in love to heal that man, despite its being detrimental to further ministry in synagogues. He may leave 99 perfectly healthy sheep alone so that he can search for one who is sick and rebellious. Such a man will indeed fall into the very pit of death, caught up in love for

---

[110] Pieper, *What does it mean to philosophize?*, 35.

God, his Father. And his impracticality will win the mockery and scorn of worldly onlookers. "Get down from there!" they will jeer. "Keep healing and everything; only do it in a way that is permitted by worldly powers."

For the one who wants to see God, who wants to orient his life towards this beatific vision and so radiate the "splendor of truth," everything ultimately depends on this: what place does God have in one's life? Is He the goal for which one strives, or is He a means to the "real" goal, which is human betterment? In his book, *Jesus of Nazareth*, Pope Benedict XVI examined the temptations of Christ in the desert. In the third temptation (as articulated in Matthew's Gospel), Satan showed Jesus "all the kingdoms of the world in their magnificence, and he said to him, 'all of these I shall give to you, if you will prostrate yourself and worship me.'"[111] At first glance, this appears to be a ridiculous temptation. How could it possibly be tempting for Jesus, the Son of God, to worship Satan? Reflecting on this with remarkable insight, the late Holy Father explained,

> The tempter is not so crude as to suggest to us directly that we should worship the devil. He merely suggests that we opt for the reasonable decision, that we choose to give priority to a planned and thoroughly

---

[111] Mt 4:8-9.

organized world, where God may have his place as a private concern but must not interfere in our essential purposes.... Jesus' third temptation proves, then, to be the fundamental one, because it concerns the question as to what sort of action is expected of a Savior of the world.... What did Jesus actually bring, if not world peace, universal prosperity, and a better world? What has he brought? The answer is very simple: God. He has brought God.[112]

In Satan's third temptation, man is forced to grapple with the place God holds in his life. Surely, beholding all the violence, pain, separations, and tragedies of all the kingdoms of the world of all times in history would have awakened in Jesus a heartbreaking compassion. And Satan was offering Him the promise of a world without any of that. All He need do is make God subservient to human prosperity, which, surely is the real good and the goal of all power. God is to be placed on the examination table, His Presence verified by the light of human, pragmatic standards.

But of course, doing so necessarily removes the capacity to behold God in the world. Because what is seen in contem-

---

[112] Pope Benedict XVI, *Jesus of Nazareth: From the Baptism in the Jordan to the Transfiguration* (New York: Doubleday, 2007), 41-44.

plation exceeds the capacity of the finite mind to grasp, if one subjects the object of contemplation to human ends, he necessarily blinds himself to it. In order to perceive the Infinite God, one must sacrifice finite goods to that end. This is precisely what happens in worship, according to Pieper:

> Divine worship means the same thing where time is concerned, as the temple where space is concerned. "Temple" means… that a particular piece of ground is specially reserved, and marked off from the remainder of the land which is used either for agriculture or for habitation. And this plot of land is transferred to the estate of the gods, it is neither lived on, nor cultivated. And similarly in divine worship a certain definite space of *time* is set aside from working hours and days, a limited time, specially marked off – and like the space allotted to the temple, is not *used*, is withdrawn from all merely utilitarian ends. It is the "festival time," and it arises in this way and no other.[113]

In divine worship, man occupies himself in a time of festivity. Setting aside all earthly cares for a time, he places himself in a posture of receptivity towards a fulfillment he himself

---

[113] Pieper, *Leisure*, 67.

cannot attain. And in so doing, he opens himself to the joy of divine love.

Jesus, then, restores the world to order not by asserting his power, but by bringing God into the world. And this happens only by the sacrifice of the Cross. In a world that worships efficiency and productivity, God will be seen as too slow, too weak, and too impractical to accomplish the real task at hand in the world, which is human betterment. Prioritizing God in worship will be perceived as inimical to human progress. The crucifixion is not an accident of Christ's life. It is what subjecting human affairs to those of God looks like in a disordered world. When someone, then, struck by the arrow of divine beauty, orients his life towards the contemplation of God, he at least implicitly embraces a life of sacrificial worship.

Sacrifice: The Pattern of Love

The one who wishes to behold God in the world must prepare himself by a life of sacrifice. But this does not *primarily* mean the doing of some unpleasant, difficult thing.[114] Primarily it means subjecting what is within human power to attain to the governance of God. This is the purpose and goal of all ascetical disciplines: that one become capable of letting

---

[114] Cf. ibid., 32-33.

go of what is not God for the sake of attaining Him, despite the seeming impracticality of such an act. And this disposes one towards a life of literally unfathomable joy.

In *My Fair Lady*, the lovestruck Freddy Eynsford-Hill encounters Eliza Doolittle at a horserace and is utterly smitten by her. Swept up by longing for her presence, he sings, "I have often walked down this street before/ but the pavement always stayed beneath my feet before/ All at once am I several stories high/ knowing I'm on the street where you live…. People stop and stare, they don't bother me/ For there's nowhere else on earth that I would rather be/ Let the time go by, I won't care if I/ Can be here on the street where you live." For Freddy, walking around in love, the everyday world of practical affairs appears different, a source of beauty and enchantment. He notices the birds' call; he hears with hopeful delight every door opening along the street. Everything is upside down, seen as if for the first time. And those who are not so in love are baffled by his impractical perspective.

Likewise, a sacrificial life baffles those who are weighed down by the "important" manners of the workaday world. Submitting the not irrelevant, but lesser affairs of the workaday world to the greater good of beholding God, sacrifice gives one an "attitude of mind [not] of those who intervene, but of those who are open to everything; not of those who grab and grab hold, but of those who leave the reigns loose and who are free and easy themselves – almost like a man falling asleep, for one can only fall asleep by 'letting oneself go.'"[115] Sacrifice does not make one hard and miserable, but like Freddy, joyful, patient, and relaxed. Perhaps the lack of sleep so lamented in our age can trace its roots back to a lack of sacrificial worship, to a lack of concrete entrustment of oneself to the Divine Other.

Those who live according to the pattern of sacrificial worship, then, look like madmen in a world organized according to the principles of efficiency and productivity. In something of a personal musing, Pieper reflects on the term "manic depressive." His reflections are worth quoting at length. He says:

> The world is so set up that anyone who were to have clear insight into it could fall into an abyss of sorrow: God's own *logos*, having become man, had to die an awful and shameful death; at the end of world history there is to be world domination by evil; Thomas Aquinas says that the beatitude "blessed are those who mourn…" is appropriate to the experience of scientific knowledge. Pondering this (and we can do this without conscious reflection) we could burst into tears and experience the deepest depression – which does not have to be unrelated to reality and have no foundation. And on the other hand: reality is at the

---

[115] Ibid., 47.

same time, and in no less real a way, interwoven with salvation; it is to such an extent – and in a way which goes beyond all comprehension – carried by God's love that anyone who thinks this through very carefully could be overcome by a joy which also might seem to be without any obvious foundation and which might simply be beyond our grasp. Why is the middle position seen as "normal"?[116]

In a rather surprising manner, Pieper thus lays bare the diseased apathy of our time. Without suggesting that someone in a manic or depressive state is psychologically sound, he nonetheless calls into question the psychic soundness of everyday man. If one perceives reality as it truly is and participates in that reality, he will find himself filled with an otherworldly joy and sorrow which is quite foreign to this world. Did not even Jesus' relatives say, after all, that "He is out of his mind"?[117] It is not (or at least, not solely) the one who feels "too much" whose psychic health we should question, but the one who feels too little, for whom all is planned and calculated, and nothing is allowed to overflow. The latter, indeed,

---

[116] Pieper, "Notes 1" in *Traditional Truth, Poetry, Sacrament*, 140.

[117] Mk 3:21.

may be more out of tune with reality, more strictly illogical, than the former.

The joy of the festival – that free, lavish, uncalculated, and effusive joy made visible in celebratory rites – is only possible for one who is willing to sacrifice. Only he is capable of beholding the beauty of God in the world because only he can let go of the finite for the sake of the Infinite.

The American Difficulty

Pieper seems to suggest that this festive disposition, springing from the font of sacrificial worship and establishing the very foundation of western culture, is particularly difficult for Americans to achieve. Pieper had several occasions to travel to America, offering semesterly lectures at different universities throughout his career. And he seemed to find America something of a puzzle. On the one hand, he was amazed to see the spontaneous confidence and trust that his students exhibited. They were free and easy in their language, evidence of a people not restrained by fear. He also experienced the generosity of a rather poor student who offered to host him during a stay, and he seemed to think there was something in the American spirit that fostered such free and confident generosity.

On the other hand, Pieper was shocked by the racism and antisemitism he witnessed during his visits in the 1950's and

60's. Furthermore, both he and his wife felt keenly the isolation of American culture, so given as it was to the workaday world. But above all, "one of Pieper's abiding suspicions of American culture," writes the philosopher Austenfeld, "was what he perceived to be its inability to admit a tragic dimension to life."[118] Indeed, on one occasion, while visiting Santa Fe, Pieper saw the words, "Smile! God loves you!" painted on the side of a church. Such a thing, he said, "would be inconceivable anywhere else in the world outside America."[119] Only in America could one assume that knowledge of God's love would necessitate a cheerful countenance before the world.

Austenfeld explains:

> Americans characteristically have an unbounded confidence in the future, based on their native optimism about overcoming obstacles, their technical expertise, and their enviable record of achievements, especially when called upon to improvise under adverse circumstances. For Pieper, however, and for his interpretation of the Western tradition, two insights are axiomatic: First, man cannot control his destiny and would likely reenact the story of Babel if he tried.

---

[118] Thomas Austenfeld, "Josef Pieper's Contemplative Assent to the World," *Modern Age* 42, no. 4 (Fall, 2000): 378.

[119] Josef Pieper, *A Journey to Point Omega: Autobiography from 1964* (South Bend: St. Augustine's Press, 2020), 99.

Second, while Christians believe that history is ordered towards a salvific goal, salvation is literally beyond this world, and human history may well end in an innerworldly catastrophe – 'whether that end be called dying, defeat of the good, martyrdom, or world domination by evil' – without thereby gainsaying God's ultimate plan for a new heaven and a new earth.[120]

For Pieper, salvation comes from God and in a way that may baffle human sensitivities. This is true both for the world as a whole and for each man in particular. We do not know what the "perfection" of oneself looks like *a priori*. It is only by orienting one's life towards God that one comes to perfection. And that may look like a failure to many, even to oneself. Man may well find himself fighting *against* God even as he strives to *follow* Him if he holds on too tightly to his own idea of holiness and fulfillment.

Because of the value that Americans place on success in this world, they may find it difficult to build their lives on divine worship and on the transcendent values that flow from it. This is not to suggest that Americans cannot entrust themselves to God. In some ways, precisely because Americans have experienced such existential despair in the midst of

---

[120] Austenfeld, 379.

such worldly affluence, they may well be in a particularly privileged position to accept the Gospel precisely as good news, as news that brings genuine salvation. But the one who entrusts himself to God, who bases his life on divine worship, will find himself in a profoundly countercultural position. And he must be willing to sacrifice much for the sake of a life oriented towards God.

This is said not to disparage Americans, but to offer a word of challenge, especially in light of one of the most moving events of Pieper's life, one which expresses his own understanding of the incorruptible joy that is the foundation of the world. In 1964, Pieper's son, Thomas, was in the United States for studies. He had drifted away from his father, as well as from the faith of his father. Pieper had prayed for a "homecoming," but saw no signs of such a return of his son to his father. One day, Pieper received a phone call: "Thomas had suddenly become very ill and was in a hospital in Seattle in Washington State."[121] Thomas had suffered a cerebral hemorrhage at a campsite on the slope of Mt. Ranier.[122] Pieper immediately booked a flight to Washington for the next morning. But before the night was over, he received the news that his son had died.

---

[121] Josef Pieper, *Not Yet the Twilight: An Autobiography 1945-1964* (South Bend: St. Augustine's Press, 2017), 289.

[122] Cf. ibid, 290.

Tragedy had thrust itself upon Pieper even from America, from a land that "does not admit a tragic dimension to life." And yet this tragedy brought him unexpected consolation. Two days after receiving news of his son's death, Pieper received a letter from Thomas which had been written shortly before he died. "This letter," wrote Pieper, "had a new tone which had long since been missing between us; suddenly I could hear the language of trust, of devotion, of humor; very early forms of address were there again as if a matter of course. Clearly it had been necessary to travel to the other side of the world to make this return possible."[123]

And yet, consoling as such a "homecoming" was, it was not this which brought Pieper the most comfort. Upon hearing of Thomas' death, one of the young man's college friends called Pieper in distress:

> He was particularly upset that he had not yet visited us and told us about Thomas, although he had been urgently asked to do so.... He said he would catch up on his visit soon; but now he wanted to say something concrete to me: his friend Thomas had gone to Mass and communion with him at Easter for the first time in a long time, and then regularly; Thomas had re-

---

[123] Ibid., 290-291.

quested him to tell us this personally, and it was very painful for him now to have done this too late.[124]

"But of course," Pieper concluded, "it was not at all 'too late.' The message about my son's homecoming – a much deeper homecoming than to his father – still came at the right time."[125] Pieper's vision of faith gave him the capacity to behold, even in the midst of unimaginable heartbreak, the joy which is the very heart of reality. "The happiness of contemplation," Pieper had written in 1957, "is a true happiness, indeed the supreme happiness, but it is founded upon sorrow."[126] In 1964, Pieper was living what he had written.

In a world that values efficiency and productivity as the highest of goods – a world, in other words, in which many Americans find themselves – it is worth asking whether such contemplative happiness is possible. Can someone who denies or distracts himself from the tragic nevertheless still embrace Ecstatic Joy as the very foundation of the world? Will not such a person close himself off from such happiness and instead settle for what can be manufactured by his own power? No matter that it fails to fulfill; it also fails to disappoint.

---

[124] Ibid., 291.
[125] Ibid., 292.
[126] Ibid.

For the Christian, however, because his life is given form by divine worship, joy comes as an unexpected and suprafulfilling gift. And only in this way does man experience the authentically human character of his existence. "I am… convinced," Pieper says, "that man is threatened by dehumanization, by the loss of his nature, the moment we cease to regard 'human nature' as something created, something designed and brought into existence by a creative mind absolutely transcendent to man."[127] The guarantor of man's humanity, of his personhood, is the capacity to offer sacrificial worship to the Creator. In so doing, man remembers that fulness of life is found in something other than what he himself can produce. Only if man can suffer the pain of finite loss can he also suffer the joy of Infinite Love. Setting apart created realities for divine worship, man remembers that only the Infinite can satisfy him.

Festivity and an Authentic Humanity

And so we come at last to the theme of festivity, the highest achievement and fullest expression of humanity. If creation is intended to be the dwelling place of divinity, and if the Divine Nature is nothing other than Eternal Joy in a

---

[127] Josef Pieper, "Human Nature and the Created State" in *Problems of Modern Faith*, 287-288.

Trinitarian Communion of Persons, then creation is most fully itself in its own expression of joyful communion. In festive celebration, "the world, for once," finds itself "in perfect harmony with all its living things."[128] Or, as Pieper says, "everyday things unexpectedly take on the freshness of Eden; the world… in Goethe's words, is 'glorious as on the first of days.'"[129] In festivity, creation speaks again of the glory of God. It speaks of the Face gazing lovingly upon it, delighting in its sheer existence. It is fully itself.

According to Pieper, "to celebrate a festival means: to live out, for some special occasion and in an uncommon manner, the universal assent to the world as a whole."[130] God is forever gazing upon His creation, giving it meaning and existence by His knowledge and love. In this way, the world's goodness is permanent and everlasting. Despite the disharmony caused by sin, the created world remains fundamentally good and capable of speaking of God.

This fundamental harmony, however, is often obscured. In the busyness of the workaday world, man can easily forget creation's role in making visible the Invisible Creator. In festivity, then, creation is freed to be itself by taking up everything earthly into the praise of God. This is not to say that

---

[128] Elton John, "Can you feel the love tonight" in *The Lion King*.
[129] Pieper, *In Tune with the World*, 39.
[130] Ibid., 30.

every feast must be explicitly religious. Rather, it means that if something is a true festival, what is celebrated is the inherent goodness and meaningfulness of creation.[131] Festive joy does not arise from a finite source. No one can attain it by affirming a thing's "usefulness." Rather, it springs from within the one who beholds the inherent beauty of creation, revealing, as it does, the Beauty of the Creator. Only if man affirms the goodness and beauty of creation as an icon of God's Goodness and Beauty can he celebrate with joy the festive occasion.

This overflowing joy of the festival gives birth to that which is most humane in our lives: "Wherever festivity can freely vent itself in all its possible forms, an event is produced that leaves no zone of life, worldly or spiritual, untouched."[132] Everything human – food, dance, song, pleasing sights and smells – is elevated in authentic festivity because man wants to make everything he can touch speak of the goodness of the Creator. The proper home and the birthplace of the arts is the festival.[133] "A feast without song and music," Pieper says, "without the visible form and structure of a ritual, without

---

[131] Cf. Pieper, *In Tune with the World*, 26.
[132] Ibid., 34.
[133] Cf. Pieper, "Work, Spare Time, and Leisure" in *Only the Lover Sings*, 25.

imagery and symbol – such a thing cannot be conceived."[134] That which is most humane in man finds its source in the wasteful abundance of festive celebration.

Because of this, whenever "we choose to give priority to a planned and thoroughly organized world," the life-breath of festivity is suffocated. Festivity lives only on the contemplative awareness of God. Whenever the experience of God is absent, festive celebration degrades itself into sham entertainment. This is not to suggest that there is anything wrong with entertainment. We need "escapes" on occasion; opportunities to relax from the heaviness of life's burdens. But without the foundation of the festival, the joys and sorrows of humanity can plunge no deeper than the surface of man's existential awareness. Only the festival gives expression to the love that is at the very heart of reality. And where the festival is no longer celebrated, human experience is necessarily more shallow.

Conclusion

In the second chapter, we saw Pieper's articulation of the man whose humanity has been formed by the contemplative awareness of God. Directing his life towards the vision of

---

[134] Pieper, "Three Talks in a Sculptor's Studio" in *Only the Lover Sings*, 68.

God, man finds himself in inner harmony, his various desires and appetites all working together for the good. Here we see all of creation being harmonized in praise of God. Not only is man to be transfigured by the vision of God; rather, all of creation is to be transfigured. By offering sacrificial worship to the Creator, man frees all of creation from its slavery to the utilitarian, pragmatic world. And in this, man tastes here on earth the joy that awaits him in the Eternal Banquet. Subjecting what is of earth to that which is of Heaven, man opens himself to receive the joy of Divine Love. And so living in love, man discovers, or re-discovers, his authentic humanity.

Conclusion

Shortly before her death, Pieper's mother asked him a question: What, she wondered, was her real name? "When she was told her first name," Pieper recalls, "she replied that she knew that one herself; it was that 'other' name that she could no longer remember."[135] While she seemed to be referring to her maiden name, Pieper uses this exchange to reflect on the transient nature of names given on earth. For no name given on earth fully and "precisely designates that which we truly are."[136] The person is too much a mystery to be encompassed with a finite name. Only in Heaven will we receive that name which fully expresses our identity.[137] Only when we see God will we truly know who and what we are in the Light of his Eternal Glory.

If we lose the capacity to perceive the Infinite, we will lose the capacity to rightly perceive the finite. And on this side of Heaven, the Infinite is perceived more in darkness than in light. That is, what we *see* in this world is the finite, created reality presented to our senses. The Infinite appears, not to our senses, but to that part of us that awakens whenever the

---

[135] Josef Pieper, "What is my Real Name?" in *Problems of Modern Faith*, 294.
[136] Ibid., 295.
[137] Cf. Is 62:2 and Rev 2:17.

finite fails to satisfy us. "The terrible thing," Pieper says, quoting Andre Gide, "is that we can never make ourselves drunk enough."[138] Our experience of the finite necessarily inclines us towards the Infinite. And the man who fills himself with the finite in an attempt to avoid his longing to behold the Infinite will find himself hopelessly frustrated. It is only by suffering the limitedness of creation that one can perceive the Infinite – God – in the world.

Most intimately, it is only by experiencing *himself* as a limited creature that man is able to experience God in himself. It is not by exalting himself that man participates in the life of God, not by autonomously defining himself and thus making a name for himself, but by emptying himself in love according to the truth. By freely *following* his natural bent in the right way, man experiences the life of God within him. He is attuned to the "movement of total reality" and so finds himself at home in the world.

The life of the Christian is thus profoundly attractive. In a world where complaints about feeling "alienated" from the world and others abound, the inner harmony of man with reality offered by Christ appears more and more beautiful. It is deadening to cut ourselves off from our created nature, from the experience of being held in existence by the Creator

---

[138] Andre Gide, quoted in Pieper, *Happiness and Contemplation*, 17.

at every moment. To do so reduces man's life on earth either to a hopeless search for self-given meaning, or to a tense obsession with external rules in the hopes that they will give stability to the goodness of his existence. Neither offers the attractiveness of a life whose meaning is given in the gaze of the Divine Lover.

What is at stake here, ultimately, is man's capacity to experience himself as a person, as someone who lives in a world of practical, utilitarian affairs, yet who, at the same time, transcends that world. Man's ultimate fulfillment comes in the beholding of God. When he remembers that, he beautifies even the mundane, earthly realities with which he daily works, so that they, too, may direct him towards God. Life becomes more humane, more personal, when it is oriented towards God in worship.

Without such orientation, man's personal dignity is threatened by imprisonment within the utilitarian world. Pieper says, "the realm of freedom, that realm constituted by *theoria* [the beholding of things for their own sake, and not for some utilitarian benefit], has no ability to maintain itself against the demonic force of the will to power, which strives to make the whole of reality a field of raw material for the exploitation of utilitarian plans…. *unless it places itself in a special way in the protection of the gods* [as the ancient Roman formulation says]."¹³⁹ Only by offering sacrificial worship to the Creator can the festive joy of the contemplative and the experience of authentic humanity be preserved.

In C.S. Lewis' *The Last Battle*, Lucy returns to us after some time away from our consciousness. We meet her in something of a stable with some others who had thought that they were being thrown into this shelter to be sacrificed. They expected to be killed. Yet they find, instead, that the inside of the stable is bigger, more alive, and more beautiful than the outside of the stable. Indeed, an entire world is within. Lucy, soaking in the mystery, recalls, "in our world, too, a Stable once had something inside it that was bigger than our whole

---

¹³⁹ Josef Pieper, "Was Heisst Akademisch?" in *Was Heisst Akademisch? Zwei Versuche über die Chance der Universität heute* (Munich: Kösel-Verlag, 1952),36. "…der Bereich der Freiheit, wie er durch die *theoria* konstituiert wird, nicht behauptet werden kann gegen die dämonische Aufsaugungsgewalt eines Machtwillens, der den Gesamtbestand des Wirklichen zum Feld und Rohstoff von Nutzungsplänen zu machen strebt… *es sei denn, sie begebe sich auf besondere Weise in den Schutz der Götter.*" I have chosen to translate this myself, because the English translation by Dan Farrelly translates Pieper's "dämonische" as "daimonic," a somewhat more neutral term for an inspiring spirit in Greek. Pieper, however, shortly after referring to this "dämonische" force, later refers to the "daimonische" spirits, the muses, which Farrelly also translates as "daimonic". It seems to me, therefore, that Pieper's decision to use these two different words is deliberate and should be translated accordingly.

world."[140] Sacrificial worship, the surrendering of the created world to the Creator, does not limit man's existence. Rather, it opens him to the Infinite. What took place in Bethlehem continues in the Church by means of her sacramental nature. Creation is a sign. It points to something more. Pieper invites us to participate in the sacramental nature of the Church by the celebration of the sacred mysteries and so become capable of finding God in the world.

---

[140] C.S. Lewis, *The Last Battle*, 744.

www.ingramcontent.com/pod-product-compliance
Lightning Source LLC
Chambersburg PA
CBHW070851050426
42453CB00012B/2146